THE OFFICIAL®

PRICE GUIDE TO

American Stoneware

THE OFFICIAL®

PRICE GUIDE TO

American Stoneware

George Sullivan

FIRST EDITION

HOUSE OF COLLECTIBLES · NEW YORK

Important Notice. All of the information, including valuations, in this book has been compiled from the most reliable sources, and every effort has been made to eliminate errors and questionable data. Nevertheless, the possibility of error, in a work of such immense scope, always exists. The publisher will not be held responsible for losses which may occur in the purchase, sale, or other transaction of items because of information contained herein. Readers who feel they have discovered errors are invited to *write* and inform us, so they may be corrected in subsequent editions. Those seeking further information on the topics covered in this book are advised to refer to the complete line of *Official Price Guides* published by the House of Collectibles.

Published by: House of Collectibles
201 East 50th Street
New York, New York 10022

Distributed by Ballantine Books, a division of Random House, Inc., New York, and simultaneously in Canada by Random House of Canada Limited, Toronto.

All photographs by Aime LaMontagne, Palmer, MA,
unless otherwise noted.

Cover design by Kristine V. Mills
Cover photo by George Kerrigan, courtesy of Harmer Rooke Galleries
Text design by Holly Johnson

Manufactured in the United States of America

Library of Congress Catalog Card Number: 93-77589
ISBN: 0-876-37894-7

First Edition: June 1993

10 9 8 7 6 5 4 3 2 1

Contents

AN OVERVIEW OF AMERICAN STONEWARE

AMERICAN STONEWARE LISTINGS

RESOURCES

Acknowledgments

I am grateful to the many collectors and dealers who contributed advice and information for this book. Special thanks are due those who permitted items from their collections to be photographed. These individuals include Charles G. Moore, Director, Harmer Rooke Galleries, New York, NY; Willard E. Grande, Regent Street Antique Center, Saratoga Springs, NY; Jack and Pat McMackin, Nine Fires Antiques, Stow, MA; Brad Maxwell, Melissa's Antiques, Dedham, MA; Betty and Joel Schatzberg, Riverside, CT; Clarence Pico, Litchfield Auction Gallery, Litchfield, CT; George Shahady, Shahady's Antiques, Bridgeport, WV; Dale Farrell, Bolton, NY; Ed and Diane Faria, Peppercricket Farm, Middleboro, MA; Tracy Law, The Curiosity Shop, Sherburne, NY; and Earl Curry, Easton, MA.

Special thanks also to Aime LaMontagne for his excellent photos, and to Larry LaMontagne; Roy Hebert; Cliff Busekit; Marlin Denlinger, Morrisville, VT; Francesca Kurti, TLC Labs, New York, NY; Steve Leder, Cheshire, CT; Mallory Max, Sotheby's; and Bill and Mary Mazens/Sullivan.

THE OFFICIAL®

PRICE GUIDE TO

American Stoneware

An Overview of American Stoneware

Introduction

Year in and year out, American salt-glazed, decorated stoneware continues to grow in popularity as a fascinating area of collectibles. From New York to California, stoneware fanciers descend upon roadside antique shops, pursue dealers, and crowd auction galleries in search of attractive and unusual crocks, jugs, jars, and other treasures.

Stoneware is a type of pottery produced from a special clay that is fired only once, but at such intense heat that it becomes vitrified, that is, very hard and nonporous. Stoneware pieces did not require glaze to be usable, but almost without exception salt was thrown into the kiln to give the ware a glossy finish and an impervious coating, thereby increasing its utility. Most pieces were decorated with a pigment containing an oxide of cobalt, deep blue in color.

Much of the pleasure to be derived from collecting stoneware comes from its social history. Before home canning or ice refrigerators (ice boxes), stoneware vessels were desperately needed by the pioneer homemaker for food storage. She required stoneware crocks for storing butter, lard, eggs, salted meats, and cucumbers and other pickled foods. She needed jugs for wine and vinegar, and for cider and molasses. In the kitchen were stoneware butter churns and batter jugs, bottles and jars, pitchers, bowls, and beanpots; in the barnyard were waterers and poultry fountains.

Stoneware gives us insight into how Americans lived a century ago, and even earlier. From it we can learn facts about past everyday life that can never be derived from a history book.

In 1807, or perhaps earlier, the firm of Warne & Letts operated a stoneware pottery in South Amboy, New Jersey, which drew upon the nearby clay deposits. About all that is known of this pottery and its production is derived from a crudely potted stoneware crock once owned by a Staten Island collector. On one side it bears the inscription WAYNE & LETTS, 1807, which was impressed into the wet clay with wooden type. On the opposite side is the inscription LIBERTY FOR EV S. AMBOY. NE JER'SY. At the time, the United States was being provoked into a second war with Great Britain, the War of 1812. The patriotic sentiment expressed by the South Amboy vessel is a reminder of that period—it is a historical document.

Many stoneware pieces have aesthetic appeal as folk art. Decorating was often done by itinerant artists who used cobalt, a dark blue metallic oxide that fired to a glasslike finish. Applied with a slip cup or stiff brush, it made possible a wide range of unusual and elaborate designs.

Collectors pay high prices for stoneware featuring rare and handsome decoration. The number of people who will pay more than $10,000 for a piece has "increased dramatically" within the past few years, according to Betty and Joel Schatzberg, well-known Connecticut folk art dealers. The auction record for a piece of stoneware is $148,500, the amount paid for an extremely rare, elaborately decorated salt-glazed inkwell auctioned at Sotheby's, New York, on June 27,

Crocks, jugs, and butter churns are among the most popular stoneware pieces.

1991. Heart-shaped in form with a beaded edge and incised flower and leaf motifs filled with cobalt blue, the inkwell was signed on the bottom NEW YORK, JULY 12, 1773, WILLIAM CROLIUS. At the time, it was the earliest dated piece of stoneware known to exist.

Most collectors, of course, content themselves with the lower end of the market, paying $300 to $500 for pieces featuring stylized birds, simple floral designs, or geometric patterns. There are many thousands of such pieces available.

Many stoneware collectors also specialize in pieces produced by a particular potter or group of potters. If you live in or near Boston, for example, it makes sense to concentrate on the stoneware produced by Jonathan Fenton, which is periodically offered for sale by antique dealers throughout most of New England. By asking questions and doing some investigation on your own, you can become a Jonathan Fenton expert.

A century or so ago, stoneware served so many utilitarian functions that it was taken for granted, like burlap or bar soap. It was gradually replaced by glass and other materials, and its use declined with advances in food preservation. Like countless other nineteenth-century objects, stoneware pieces are now regarded as antiques.

For the stoneware collector, therefore, this book should

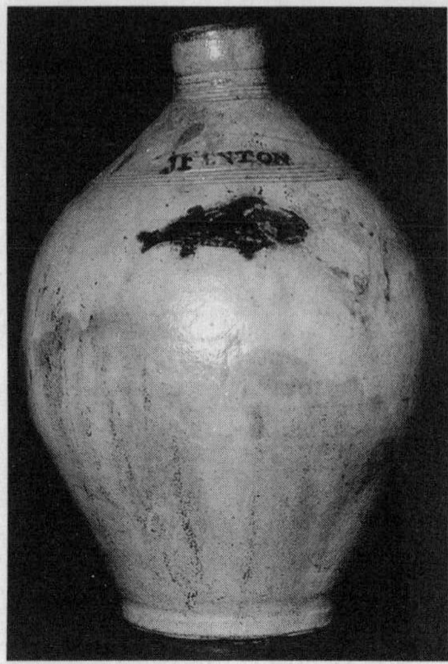

This handsome ovoid whiskey jug is the work of Boston potter Jonathan Fenton.

prove a useful aid. It examines stoneware history, explains how pieces were manufactured and decorated, and gives tips on buying and selling. There's a comprehensive list of stoneware potters and potteries in the chapter titled "Resources," and more than 150 photographs illustrate a wide range of stoneware forms and decorations.

Almost any piece of stoneware in decent condition with just the slightest touch of cobalt blue is worth something. Those who seek to buy stoneware for investment purposes, therefore, will also find this book useful. So, too, will those who wish to build a collection of objects that can be personally rewarding and provide a lifetime of satisfaction and pleasure.

Looking Back

Stoneware's roots are European, not American. Early in the fourteenth century, mottled brown stoneware was being produced by potteries in the Rhine Valley of Germany and France. Not only were durable tankards, mugs, storage vessels, and other utilitarian pieces being created, but also ornamental and decorated vessels.

As early as 1520, Rhenish potters in and around Frechen were making a type of stoneware jug that featured the molded portrait of a grim-faced bearded figure on the neck. In sizes ranging from one pint to about five gallons in capacity, it was called a bartman jug, bartman meaning "bearded man." A century or so later, with the Reformation engulfing much of central and western Europe, Cardinal Robert Bellarmino of Italy was sent to the Low Countries in an effort to stem the tide. His presence there was deeply resented. Because of Bellarmino's resemblance to the visage on the bartman jug, including the very same "cathedral cut" beard, people began

This one-pint bellarmine jug, once a part of the Georgeanna Greer collection, dates to the late eighteenth or early nineteenth century.

calling the jugs "bellarmines," and the term has endured to this day.

During the seventeenth century, Rhenish ware, the most durable pottery available, was exported to other nations of Europe, including England. British potters began to imitate what was being produced in the Rheinland, turning out fine tableware and as well as decorative pieces. John Dwight, one of the best known of the early English potters, obtained a patent to produce salt-glazed stoneware at his shop in Fulham in 1671. By the middle of the eighteenth century, salt-glazed stoneware was being manufactured in England in large quantities for shipment to the American colonies.

When New York City was established in 1625 as New Amsterdam, it's probably safe to assume that among the early Dutch settlers clustered at the lower end of Manhattan Island were a number who had a practical knowledge of pottery making. Early records show this to be true. A list of burghers for the "City of Amsterdam, New Netherland," dated April 18, 1657, contains the name of Dirck Clasen, "pot-Baker." It is not known, however, whether Clasen practiced the potter's craft in New Amsterdam. No record of any Clasen pottery exists.

The same holds true for John Dewilde, "Pottmaker," Dirck Benson, "Pott Baker," and John Euwatse, "Pottmaker." These three are listed as freemen of the city of New York, 1697–98. But, again, there are no records of any pottery owned or operated by any of the three, and no pottery specimens attributed to them have ever been recovered.

Historians and archeologists have established that a pottery was operating at Burlington, New Jersey, as early as 1684. While no examples of its output have ever been recovered, it is known to have produced a white, fine-textured, salt-glazed stoneware.

Dr. Daniel Coxe of London founded the Burlington enterprise. A one-time governor of West New Jersey, Coxe never made the crossing to America but acted through an agent and his son, Daniel Coxe, Jr. Regarding what may have been one of America's first successful potteries, therefore, historians not only knew the name of the owner but have also established its approximate location, the name of the manager, and the names of at least two of the potters. Two kilns were kept operating at the Burlington site, whose resulting products were called "white and chiney ware." The output was substantial enough to permit Coxe to export pieces to the Barbados and Jamaica. "It is well within the bounds of possibility," says John Spargo in *Early American Pottery and China*, "that reposing on the shelves of some collectors today are specimens of white-glazed stoneware, attributed to seventeenth century England, and so classified, which were actually made in the Coxe pottery at Burlington, New Jersey."

The earliest examples of American stoneware showed a close relationship to Rhenish and English forms. Typically, German-American potters produced long-neck jugs, bulbous jars, and heavily banded cylindrical mugs. They were noted for ornate decoration often achieved by brushing a cobalt solution into an incised design beneath the salt glaze. They were also skilled in natural clay and slip glazes.

By comparison, the early British potters in America were somewhat restrained. They produced simple cylindrical jars and short-necked jugs. The usual technique for decoration involved dipping the upper and sometimes lower portions of the vessel into an often brownish or rust-colored mixture before firing, which produced a contrasting band at the top and/or bottom. Sometimes incised bands were also used as decoration.

William Crolius—who was born in Coblenz, Germany, in 1700 and emigrated to New York City in 1718—was one of the earliest American stoneware artisans. It is not known exactly when he opened his pottery, but by 1730 it was in operation at the foot of Pottbaker's Hill in Manhattan.

After William Crolius died, his son, John, and later his grandson, Clarkson, continued the operation of the Crolius Pottery. In 1812, when Potter's Hill was leveled and the fill used to obliterate Collect Pond, Clarkson Crolius moved the family pottery to 65 Bayard Street. There the business operated until 1848.

William Crolius and his descendants were New York potters for more than a century and a half. This whiskey jug bearing the Crolius imprint dates to about 1820.

Clarkson Crolius was a man of some importance in New York City. From 1802 to 1805, he was an assistant alderman from the Sixth Ward, a position his father had also held. Clarkson Crolius served as a member of the New York Assembly from 1806 to 1807 and again from 1818 to 1825. An influential member of the Democratic Party, he laid the cornerstone for Tammany Hall on May 13, 1811.

Sometime before the death of Clarkson Crolius, the ownership and control of the pottery passed to his son, Clarkson Crolius II, and the business continued to operate until 1887. Today, stoneware vessels are occasionally bought and sold bearing the imprint C. CROLIUS, MANUFACTURER, NEW YORK. Should such pieces be attributed to Clarkson Crolius I or II? No one can say for certain. The Crolius "heart'" inkwell, however, described in the introduction to this book, is the only known piece to be signed and dated by Crolius I. It may, according to the Sotheby's catalog, "possibly represent the apex of this highly skilled craftsman's career."

John Remmey, from Neuweid, Germany, was another early potter. He established his pottery in New York City about 1735, choosing a site near Crolius. (The first John Remmey died in 1762 and was succeeded by his son, John Remmey II.) Some of the more than 200-year-old pieces manufactured by Crolius and Remmey can be seen in the collection of the New York Historical Society and the Metropolitan Museum of Art in New York City.

Jonathan Durell was another prominent eighteenth-century New York City potter. He first set up shop in 1753, closed the business, then began operating again in 1774. From contemporary advertisements, it's known that Durell informed prospective customers that his output was "far superior in generality, and equal to the best of any imported from Philadelphia, or elsewhere." He offered an impressive array of stoneware pieces, including "butter, water, pickle, and oyster pots; porringers, milk pans of several sizes; jars of several sizes; quart and pint mugs; quart, pint, and half bowls of various colors; small cups of various shapes; striped and coloured dishes of divers colours; pudding pans and wash basins; sauce pans, and a variety of other sorts of ware, too tedious to particularize."

Today, pre–nineteenth-century New York City pieces are occasionally offered by dealers and auction houses. "It's a small market, a finicky market," says Joel Schatzberg. "Those pieces that are heavily decorated and signed can bring astronomical prices. An early Crolius with a fish design, for example—well, you can put about any price on it."

John Pierce, who is known to have operated a pottery in Litchfield in 1753, is believed to be the earliest of Connecticut's potters. Two of his contemporaries, Jesse Washams and Hervey Brooks, had potteries in or near Litchfield. These men turned out the simplest redware and possibly some stoneware. It's generally believed that John Norton, Vermont's pioneer potter, learned the trade at the Litchfield potteries.

The Revolutionary War, by cutting off the importation of goods from England, served as a stimulus to American potteries. No longer did they have to compete with British imports. The market was theirs alone, and the demand was never greater. With no English earthenware available, native potters were called upon to provide jars and jugs, crocks and churns, milk pans and pitchers, and other wares for the kitchen and dairy. While domestic pieces might not have been the equal of British pieces in terms of workmanship and appearance, they served the purpose. When the war ended, the return of peace and a sense of independence energized American commerce and industry. Pottery making grew by leaps and bounds, and quality improved.

During this period, brown stoneware began to give way to gray. These pieces were glazed directly over the clay and often decorated with the now familiar cobalt-oxide blue glaze, which was brushed onto the surface.

Some pieces, however, were a blend of the two traditions. The output of the Boston pottery of Jonathan Fenton and

Frederick Carpenter between 1793 and 1797 is a case in point. Both men were born in America of British parents and both worked with potters in New Haven, Connecticut, before founding their own works in Boston. Fenton's work often shows Germanic influence. Long-necked, full-bodied jugs with incised designs are typical. Carpenter's work was more British. He used brown ferrugenous dips on the upper and lower portions of his pots. The vessels bore the name BOSTON in impressed letters, the result of a stamp (stamping being an American innovation).

Thomas Commeraw established a pottery at Corlears Hook in New York City about 1797. His pieces were often decorated with incised floral designs, a style of decoration frequently used by New York City potters of the late eighteenth and early nineteenth centuries. James Morgan, who was active in Cheesequake, New Jersey, late in the eighteenth century, became, like Commeraw, a potter whose works are highly valued today.

About 1790, Nathaniel Seymour established a pottery in Hartford, Connecticut, employing four men as potters. He was convinced that Connecticut clay was as good as any from Long Island, New Jersey, or anywhere else, and relied on it exclusively. Seymour used a glaze made of lead oxides mixed with local sand, and decorated his pieces with somewhat crude designs done in cobalt blue. Nathaniel Seymour retired about 1825 and the operation of his pottery was carried on by his grandson, Major Seymour, until 1842.

At about the same time Nathaniel Seymour was setting up shop, John Soutar, an Englishman, was establishing another Hartford pottery. This operation continued until 1805, when Soutar sold to Peter Cross.

As early as 1792, Charles Northrup was turning out salt-glazed stoneware and redware at Norwich, Connecticut. A number of pieces marked NORWICH that bear dates from 1794 to 1812 are attributed to him.

The first pottery in Vermont was started by Captain John Norton, a Revolutionary War veteran, in Bennington. Norton settled there in 1785. Vermont, which did not enter the Union until 1791, was practically an independent republic at the time.

Norton operated a distillery as well as a large farm in Bennington, and in 1793 he established a pottery on the farm to meet his needs and those of the community (Bennington was the largest settlement in Vermont at the time). His pottery produced milk pans, cider jugs, butter jars, platters, and plates. He made only redware at first, but before long he added salt-glazed stoneware to his output.

The Norton pottery continued to produce stoneware until 1823 or 1824. He used no pottery mark during his lifetime, but a number of pieces known to have been produced at the pottery during its earliest years have found their way into museum and historical society collections.

John Norton was succeeded in 1823 by his son, Luman Norton. A decade later, when the pottery moved to a new site in what was then called East Bennington, Luman Norton, together with his son, Julius, were the proprietors. The pottery was well known for the high quality of its jugs, churns, and other such products.

When Julius Norton assumed full control of the business in 1841, he broadened the product line to include Rockingham ware. While there is some confusion about this term, in this case it refers to the glazed brown and yellow mottled earthenware pitchers, pie plates, teapots, and other such household objects made at Bennington and hundreds of other American products potteries. (Rockingham ware can also allude to a type of early and elegant English porcelain.)

Jonathan Fenton, who founded a pottery at Dorset, Vermont, in 1801, also, like John Norton, established a family tradition for the craft. The Dorset pottery was operated by Fenton and his sons, Richard Lucas Fenton and Christopher Webber Fenton, until about 1834.

Christopher Fenton married the sister of Julius Norton, and in 1844 the two brothers-in-law formed a partnership. Norton & Fenton stayed in business until mid-1847. While

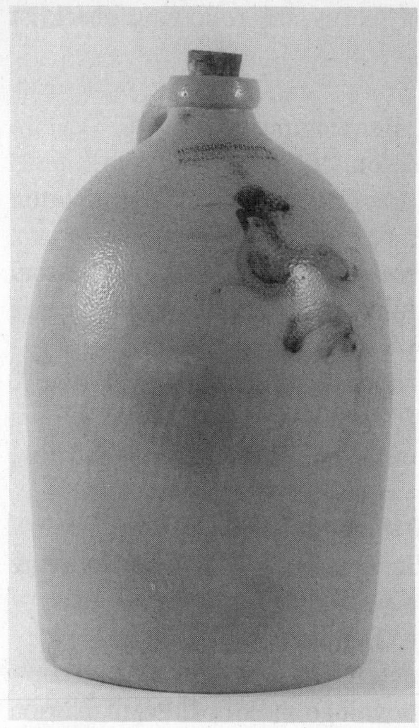

The Norton and Fenton names were linked on this two-gallon jug, produced between 1845 and 1847.

stoneware was the company's chief product, Norton & Fenton also produced Rockingham ware.

Christopher Fenton brought artisans of great skill to Bennington, including Daniel Greatbach, who had been a designer and modeler in Jersey City. Greatbach was to win his greatest acclaim while in Fenton's employ.

The Norton potteries continued to operate until 1894, producing ware of the highest quality. As John Spargo says in *Early American Pottery and China*, ". . . the pottery produced by the several generations of descendants of Captain John Norton, within the limits of that class of ware, has never been excelled in this country."

Marks used by the various Norton potteries in Bennington usually took the form of stamped lettering, with no ornamentation of any kind. They occupied two lines, with the firm name above the words "Bennington, Vt."

In seeking to date Norton pieces, the following checklist can be consulted:

1823–28: L. Norton & Co., Bennington, VT
1823–33: L. Norton, Bennington, VT
1833–40: L. Norton & Son, East Bennington, VT; L. Norton & Son, Bennington, VT
1841–44: Julius Norton, East Bennington, VT; J. Norton, East Bennington, VT; Julius Norton, Bennington, VT; J. Norton, Bennington, VT
1844–47: Norton & Fenton, East Bennington, VT; Norton & Fenton, Bennington, VT
1847–50: J. Norton, Bennington, VT; Julius Norton, Bennington, VT
1850–59: J. & E. Norton, Bennington, VT
1859–61: J. Norton & Co., Bennington, VT; J. & E. Norton & Co., Bennington, VT
1861–81: E. & L. P. Norton, Bennington, VT
1881–83: E. Norton, Bennington, VT
1883–94: Edward Norton, Bennington, VT; Edward Norton & Co., Bennington, VT; E. Norton & Co., Bennington, VT; Edward Norton & Company, Bennington, VT
1886–94: Edward Norton Company, Bennington VT

Besides Norton pottery, a good number of collectors in the Northeast specialize in the pottery of Noah White, whose name is seen frequently on crocks and jugs with bird and flower designs. White's stoneware was manufactured from the 1830s until the turn of the century, and even beyond. When it ceased operation in 1907, White's of Utica, New York, ranked as the largest pottery in the state, and its output was distributed throughout most of the United States as far as California.

Noah White left his home in Thetford, Vermont, in 1820 to settle in Vernon, New York. By 1828 he was living in Utica, and in 1834 he was listed in a city directory as a "stoneware manufacturer at Addington's." Sometime before

1840, White purchased Addington's as well as a small adjacent operation to become Utica's only potter.

Working with his sons Nicholas and, later, William, White produced pottery that was generally ovoid in shape and had simple, often crudely done decoration. Each vessel's capacity in gallons was given and the pieces were imprinted N. WHITE/UTICA.

Noah White's two sons became his partners in 1849 and the company's imprint was changed to read WHITE'S/UTICA, WHITES'/UTICA, or WHITES/UTICA. Punctuation, obviously, was not one of the firm's strong points. When Noah White died in 1865, Nicholas took over the business.

Over the next twenty years, WHITES/UTICA was the imprint used most often. Jugs and crocks of this period were straight-sided, not ovoid. They were topped with distinctive collars and the designs were more carefully rendered. Birds and flowers continued to be the usual themes.

A price list reprinted in the *Stoneware Collector's Journal* indicates the wide range of White's output. The firm offered jugs (including special molasses jugs), churns, pitchers, spit-

One of the White potteries produced this three-gallon jug around 1850.

toons, flowerpots, cream pots, batter pots (with covers), preserve jars (also with covers), beer bottles, inkstands, and stove tubes.

White's enjoyed its greatest success during the 1870s. A new building was added and a steam engine installed. No longer was hand throwing necessary, thanks to steam-powered turning wheels and molds.

Because the company's products were distributed so widely, the firm added N.Y. to its imprint. From about the year 1876, the mark read WHITE'S/UTICA, N.Y.

Although White's was producing more pottery than ever before, the quality did not suffer. Their designs became notable for the intensity of the cobalt blue. A pamphlet published in 1888 that described the industries of Utica hailed White's for its decorated pottery, and reported that the company manufactured its own coloring and kept the process a secret. "Much trouble has been experienced by potters generally in this country in obtaining suitable color for their wares," the pamphlet noted. "So great indeed has this difficulty been, that some potteries have dispensed with the decorations entirely, sending their goods to market perfectly plain. This firm, however, manufactures their own coloring composition after a process known only to themselves, and though frequently offered five times the price per pound asked in the open market for ordinary potter's blue, they decline to dispose of any, but give their customers the benefit of their investigation in the way of more desirable goods at no advance in prices."

Charles N. White, a grandson of Noah, took over the operation of the firm in the 1880s. During most of the decade that followed, White's was known as the Central New York Pottery. From 1899 to 1906, it became White's Pottery again.

By that time, White's was facing stiff competition from the availability of glass containers. In response to a diminishing demand for standard stoneware products, White's began manufacturing and selling fire brick, furnace brick, and oven tile. But these and other products that the company sought to sell could not prevent what was probably inevitable. The company stopped manufacturing stoneware in 1907, continuing in business as Charles N. White Clay Products Co. White shut down completely in 1910.

According to an article by Barbara Franco that appeared in the *Stoneware Collector's Journal*, White's went through the following stages:

Noah White 1834–1848
Noah White & Sons 1849–1856
N. White & Son 1857–1863
Noah White, Son & Co. 1864–1865
N. A. White & Co. 1866
N. A. White & Son 1867–1878
N. A. White 1878–1882
N. A. White & Son 1882–1890
Central New York Potter 1890–1898
White's Pottery Inc. 1899–1906
Charles N. White Clay Products Co. 1907–1910

Soon after White's closed, the buildings that housed the pottery operation were torn down. About all that remains to document the existence of White's today is the pottery itself.

Decade by decade during the nineteenth century, American stoneware became more utilitarian and easier to produce. The curve of the sides flattened out, bases became wider, and rims became thicker to reduce the likelihood of chipping.

By the 1860s, crocks were straight-sided and jugs were rounded into heavily rimmed necks. Bottles were cylinders, too. Decorations were images from the potter's environment—flowers, leaves, and birds. Patriotic symbols and human figures were also used. At this time quantity was most important, not quality and, certainly, not esthetics. During its heyday, stoneware was meant to be made quickly and sold cheaply.

By the late 1860s, the demand for stoneware was beginning to ebb. Safe and reliable glass jars used for home canning had become available. During the 1870s, the ice refrigerator—or icebox—came into vogue. A stout, insulated oak cabinet with a partitioned section for ice, the icebox proved superior for cooling and preserving food and beverages.

The refrigerated transport of meat was still another innovation. No longer did the American householder have to store meat or other perishables for long periods of time. A decade later, homemakers could choose from an array of mass-produced and inexpensive glass or tin containers.

The market for salt-glazed stoneware, therefore, began to shrink. The smaller potteries and those less able to withstand the competition were the first to fail. By the 1890s, the character of the stoneware industry had undergone enormous change. The potter-craftsman had been replaced by the stoneware factory, which used mass-production techniques.

Today, collectors avidly seek the works of Norton and Seymour, Remmey and Crolius, and other skilled potters. Their crocks and jugs, which originally sold for a few dollars a dozen, now command prices that range upward to many thousands of dollars apiece.

Manufacturing

For its crocks, jugs, churns, and other products, the stoneware industry depended on fine white clay, available in only a handful of sites. Clay is a type of fine-grained earth that forms a paste when mixed with water and hardens when heated. To the potter, plasticity is a vital quality. The clay must be capable of being molded.

Dry strength is also crucial. Once molded, the clay must be able to hold its shape while drying. In fact, its dry strength must be such that the molded pieces can be handled, moved about, and stacked in the kiln.

The highest quality clay to be used in stoneware manufacture came from vast deposits in Amboy, New Jersey, and also in Pennsylvania, near Philadelphia. A somewhat poorer quality was found on Long Island. The availability of clay was the principal reason that some of the first potters located in New Jersey, in New York City, across New York harbor from Amboy, and in coastal New England, not far from the Long Island supply.

As the industry grew, it followed the navigable waterways into the interior. The potteries of Bennington, Vermont, and Fort Edward, Troy, and Albany, New York, were clustered near the Hudson River, which was used to transport clay by sloop or barge from northern New Jersey. The river was also used for the shipment of finished pottery. Nathan Clark, for example, who founded a pottery at Athens (about 30 miles south of Albany) in 1805, brought clay north from Amboy and Long Island by the sloopload. Each shipment was unloaded at Clark's own Hudson River docks.

There were exceptions, however. While Adam States of Greenwich, Connecticut, whose pottery was operating as early as 1750, relied on clay shipped to him across Long Island Sound from Huntington, Long Island, other Connecticut potters did not. Ebenezer Faxon, who founded a pottery in Hartford in 1770, used what was called "Hartford clay," which came from a large deposit that extended from Hartford to Berlin. Nathaniel Seymour, another late–eighteenth-

This four-gallon crock with its vivid rendering of a songbird is typical of the output of N. A. White & Sons, one of the many potters once located along the waterways of upstate New York.

century Hartford stoneware craftsman, who employed four potters, is said to have sworn by the high quality of Hartford clay, which he used exclusively.

The opening of the New York Barge Canal, or Erie Canal, in 1825, which linked Albany in the east with Buffalo far to the west—connecting the Hudson River and Lake Erie—gave rise to the opening of stoneware potteries in Canada and the Great Lakes region. It became standard procedure to load clay on canal barges at Amboy for shipment up the Hudson River and then to pottery makers in western New York, northern Ohio and Pennsylvania, and southern Ontario.

PREPARING THE CLAY

When the clay arrived at the potteries, it had often been in transit for several weeks, and thus was raw, unpurified, and almost completely dry. Rocks, pebbles, and hardened lumps had to be removed and the clay had to be restored to its plastic state.

These operations were performed by a machine called a pug mill. In its simplest form, the pug mill consisted of a cylinder-shaped wooden vat that was fitted with a central shaft from which wooden or metal rods or blades projected, extending almost to the inner vat wall. The shaft could be turned by a horse or a mule walking in a circle around the mill, although some mills relied on water power. The clay was loaded into the mill at the top, along with a measured amount of water. As the spiked shaft turned, it acted as a mixer, rendering the clay into a syrupy state. Some potters added local clay to the imported clay at this stage, although this could result in stoneware of inferior quality, porous and susceptible to chipping, flaking, or cracking.

The wet clay was removed from the pug mill through an opening in the base. It was then worked through screens to remove the stones, hard lumps, and other impurities. The clay was then kneaded into long, log-shaped "bolts" for storage.

Each bolt weighed about twenty pounds. Sometimes, however, it went right to the potter's wheel in its plastic state.

In small potteries, one man did virtually all the work. Large operations were specialized. There was a master potter, or thrower, who formed each piece. Apprentices prepared the clay, made balls of the proper size and weight for the thrower, and fired the kiln. Other assistants, perhaps journeymen, applied the handles or created spouts, or were dubbed finishers and completed each piece. Still others decorated.

The manufacture of stoneware was a male occupation almost exclusively. While there is evidence that women sometimes owned potteries, few, if any, worked as potters or "throwers." There was too much physical labor involved. Women, however, were sometimes employed as decorators. Donald Webster, in his book titled *Decorated Stoneware and Pottery of North America*, speaks of five different nineteenth-century potteries in New York state wherein the decoration was done by women.

The master potter took a rounded glob of clay and literally threw it so it would stick to the wheel, a rotating horizontal disk. He centered the clay upon the wheel as he turned the wheel base in a counterclockwise direction with his feet. He then began to shape the clay, using his thumbs, fingers, and palms.

The first step was to open a hole in the middle of the ball using a thumb and forefinger, forming a thick-walled cylinder. Positioning the fingers of one hand inside and those of the other hand outside, he shaped and raised the vessel's walls from the bottom, pulling in a gentle upward motion as the wheel spun. Some potters used wooden ribs or scrapers to smooth and shape. At the top, he formed a rim in the case of a crock or squeezed the clay into a neck for a jug.

It was important that the walls of the pot be of uniform thickness from top to bottom. A potter not fully skilled might turn out a vessel with thick walls near the bottom rising to thinner walls at the top. When such a vessel was fired, it heated unevenly. Then, during cooling, the thinner areas tended to crack. Too thin a bottom might also crack away from thicker walls.

The process of rough-shaping didn't take very long, perhaps two or three minutes. The thrower worked fast. After all, he was expected to turn out two or three hundred pieces in a day.

After smoothing the outer surface with a wooden rib and cutting away any excess clay from the base with a pointed tool, the vessel was cut from the wheel by drawing a length of wire under it as close to the wheel as possible. After the potter had lifted the vessel onto a drying board, he moved to another wheel where an apprentice had already placed another ball, and the process was repeated.

Another finisher might apply an impressed design in a band around the vessel near the top. The simple cog wheel was used for this purpose. As the vessel was slowly turning, the wheel was pressed into the damp surface. Notched coins or toothed gears served as early cog wheels.

Once the drying process had stiffened the vessel, handles were applied. These had been pre-formed by hand or in molds. The name of the pottery might also be impressed into the surface by means of a hand stamp at this stage.

It was usual for a potter to form a large number of vessels of the same size and type at each throwing session. Uniformity depended upon the skill of the potter, for the measuring tools he had were few. He began with a measured amount of clay. A four-pound ball was standard for a one-gallon crock or jug. When a large churn was being produced, a twenty-pound ball was used. A height gauge, a stick mounted to project over the wheel, was used to make uniform the vertical measurement of the vessel. Calipers were sometimes used for establishing the inner and outer diameters. All else beyond the vessel's height and width depended on the potter's judgment—the thickness of the vessel's bottom and sides, the type of rim, the shape of the handles, the way in which the handles were attached, and the manner in which the bottom was finished. In the absence of maker's marks, individual characteristics can sometimes be used to identify different potters representing the same area.

Drying was the next operation. In smaller potteries, the finished vessels were lined up on boards, ten to twelve pieces to a board, and carried out into the sun. In the evening, the boards had to be carried back in to an enclosed storage area. The dried, unglazed vessels, called greenware, had to be handled with great care, for they were fragile and crumbled easily. In wet weather, drying had to be done indoors. Large potteries were much more efficient, relying on drying chambers, which were, essentially, large wood-fired, low-temperature ovens.

After they had dried, the unglazed vessels were coated on the inside with a brownish clay known as Albany slip, which came from the banks of the Hudson River near that city. The slip sealed the vessel's interior. The next step was to decorate the piece.

THE FIRING PROCESS

Once dried and decorated, the vessels were ready for firing. Firing was done in a kiln, a good-sized, heavy-walled, brick-lined oven that was heated by a wood fire. Because of the extremely high temperature that was required for firing—up to 2,300 degrees Fahrenheit, white heat—the kiln had to be carefully constructed. It consisted of a firebox big enough to accommodate large amounts of wood, a firing chamber in which the vessels were placed, and a venting system that permitted heat to leave the kiln.

The firing operation usually took six or seven days. Since the kiln had to be constantly tended day and night by a skilled artisan during that period, firing was expensive. For that reason, as many pieces as possible were loaded into the kiln. The total might range from several hundred to more than a thousand, a week's output of the potter and his assistants.

Loading the kiln was an art. The vessels were stacked in

layers, with the pieces on the bottom resting on setting tiles. To keep the contact points between the vertically stacked points as small as possible, short strips of clay were placed between them. These pieces of clay, which were fired and glazed along with the pottery, could not be used again and were discarded. Today, these clay strips are often found in enormous quantities when early pottery sites are excavated.

Once loaded, the kiln was closed and the fire started. The temperature was raised gradually so as to allow the moisture within the vessels to be released slowly. If the kiln temperature built too rapidly, the moisture formed into steam that could crack the surface of the vessels. Since these cracks usually did not extend through the entire wall and the vessel could still hold liquid, they could be sold to the potter's customers. Vessels with such imperfections—called firing cracks or water cracks—are not uncommon today.

It took as long as two days to raise the kiln temperature to 2,200 or 2,300 degrees Fahrenheit, which was necessary for salt glazing. At this temperature, the kiln interior took on a dark red glow. The kilnman had no thermometer capable of telling him when the kiln was hot enough for glazing. He judged conditions by eye, watching the changing color of the pottery through a viewing hole. Throughout the firing, he had to keep the kiln temperature level. A rapid plunge could cause the pots to discolor or even crack.

In salting, the top of the kiln was opened and common rock salt was shoveled in. No precise amount was called for. Too little would not do the job; too much could damage the pots. Again, the kilnman relied on his experience. Often a bushel or so was necessary to do the job.

Upon hitting the 2,300-degree heat, the salt vaporized almost immediately. In its gaseous form, the sodium combined with the high silica content of the clay to form a hard surface coating—the glaze—on every exposed surface.

Once the glazing process was complete, the kilnman kept the fire burning and the temperature at a high level for three or four more days, or until the fusion process was complete. Then the temperature was slowly reduced. The glow within the kiln quickly faded.

Most potters were a bit secretive about their operations. Mixing recipes and kiln-operating instructions were seldom written down, but around 1835, Nathan Clark, who operated potteries in Athens and Lyons, New York, published a list of rules regarding the firing process for his employees. According to Clark:

> Have your wood in good order. Raise your fire progressively, neither too fast or too slow. Examine well and understand the management of your kiln so as to heat all parts alike. Be careful not to throw your wood in [the fire] too soon or do any other act that may have a tendency to retard the heat. When fit to glaze have your salt dry. Scatter it well in every part of the kiln. During this act you must keep a full and clear blaze so as to accelerate the glazing and give the ware a bright gloss. Stop it perfectly tight and in six days you may have a good kiln of ware.

When firing was completed, the kiln was allowed to cool. Only then could it be opened and the pots removed.

IMPERFECTIONS

Mishaps were common during the firing process, often resulting in imperfections. Such vessels were usually not thrown away, however. As long as a pot held water, it could usually be sold.

One common problem was cracking from too rapid cooling of the kiln. If the fracture penetrated the pot wall, the vessel had to be discarded. It was standard procedure for the potter to test each piece of ware by tapping it with a metal tool. If a sharp ring resulted, he could be sure the pot had no dooming crack. Serious collectors perform a similar test today, snapping a finger against a pot wall and listening for a resounding ping. Without it, the pot has to be judged as being of inferior quality.

"Slumping" was another problem. When the heat within the kiln got too high (because the kiln was overfired), the clay could soften and the pots could sag or wilt, especially in any area where more than the normal amount of weight was being supported. Sometimes, for example, a jug neck would take on a droopy look. Overfiring, however, wasn't the only reason that pots came out of the kiln misshapen. This condition also resulted when the pieces on the bottom of the stack shifted or buckled because of the weight placed upon them.

Particles of lime in the clay also sometimes burst open during the firing, pocking the surface with fingernail-size blemishes. These are called "popouts." Iron particles in the clay could also scar the vessel walls or mar them with black residue. Almost any impurity, in fact, including a tiny piece of plant or tree root excavated with the clay, could create a surface defect during the firing.

Sometimes high firing temperatures melted salt deposits that had accumulated on overhead sections of the kiln. Even kiln brick could melt if the temperature got high enough. The resulting drippings fell upon pot surfaces.

Problems in glazing also created defects. If the clay from which the vessels were formed did not contain sufficient silica, the chemical process necessary to create the glaze was disrupted. The same could happen if not enough salt was used during glazing. Such vessels were dull and dry in appearance.

Sometimes part(s) of a pot failed to receive enough vapor coating and no glaze developed. This could happen in the case of the interior wall of a vessel when its top happened to be covered in the kiln.

Blistering and peeling resulted when direct flame came in contact with a pot's outer surface. In the most serious cases, sections of the surface could be left without any glaze at all.

"Crawling" was a condition that sometimes occurred in glazes that were prepared with wood ash. Instead of being smooth and uniform, the glaze mixture would form into small clumps. Crawling, however, had no adverse effect upon the ware. When the condition was uniform, in fact, it could seem quite decorative.

"Pinholing" was another type of imperfection having to do with glazes. It occurred when the glaze mixture was not vaporous enough. After the glazing process was completed and the firing of the pottery continued, moisture would continue to escape from the clay. As it did, tiny holes in the glaze would be created. If the glaze was of the right density, there was no problem; the glaze simply melted back over the hole. But when the glaze was too thick, the tiny holes never got re-covered. The same condition could cause small surface blisters.

What is perhaps the most common glaze defect—although a minor one, to be sure—was caused by the method used to stack pots in the kiln. They were kept separated by lumps or small rolls of scrap clay. Thus, any part of a vessel

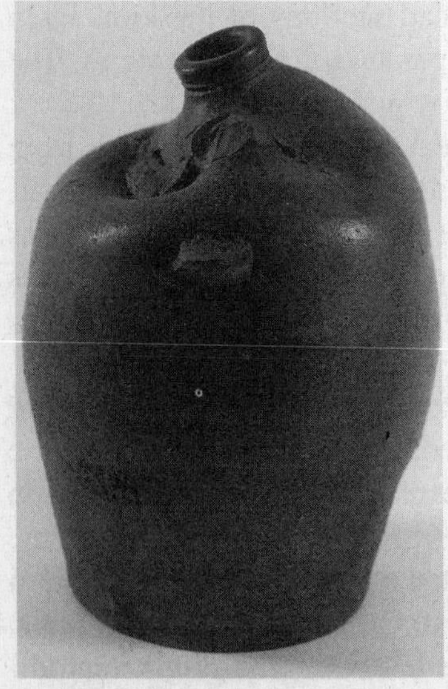

Although this one-gallon jug slumped during firing, the potter, who operated along the Ohio River in Ohio, Indiana, or Kentucky, still managed to find a customer for it.

in contact with these "separators" remained unglazed. The pot could even be scarred in that area.

Blistering, flaking, and other kiln mishaps diminish the value of a piece, as do cracks, chips, stains, and other injuries caused by use. It's not a good idea to buy anything that is damaged, even at a "bargain" price, unless you plan to keep it forever. Damaged pieces are very difficult to sell.

Despite what has previously been said, however, less-than-perfect pieces of great rarity or with exceptional decoration can still command upper-end prices, as long as the imperfection does not detract from the decoration. At a Marlin Denlinger auction not long ago, a kitchen crock fetched $13,750, despite a big crack. Generally speaking, however, condition is of prime importance whenever an appraisal is to be made.

On the other hand, don't expect stoneware pieces to be absolutely perfect. The firing process produced a wide range of imperfections, as this chapter points out. And the purchased pieces were taken into the home and used and used. When it comes to stoneware, no piece is really mint.

DISTRIBUTION

How a potter distributed his ware depended upon the size of his operation. Often a potter's output was intended to be sold within a hundred or so miles of the pottery itself, and the potter, or one or more of his employees, would sometimes transport freshly formed pieces along a regular route. Besides householders, merchants who purchased large lots at wholesale prices were the potter's customers. The potter would load a wagon, packing crocks, jugs, and other pieces in straw, and then set out. One month he might head eastward from the pottery, the next month, northward, and so on. Sometimes the distribution operation might be handled by a drummer, a traveling salesperson who owned his own wagon and purchased loads at the pottery for resale. It might also be noted that potters didn't necessarily take only cash for the pots. There was some bartering, and all types of farm produce were accepted in exchange.

In the case of large potteries, stoneware traveled by water. Barges carried the ware produced in the Albany, New York, area south along the Hudson River to New York City. As early as 1823, barges from Albany penetrated as far west as Rochester, New York, and into Lake Champlain, using the Champlain Canal. Two years later, the Erie Canal opened, linking the Great Lakes and New York.

Pottery manufactured in New York and northern New Jersey was shipped south to Charleston, South Carolina, Savannah, Georgia, and other southern Atlantic ports, as well as ports on the Gulf of Mexico. In *American Stonewares*, Georgeanna Greer notes that an inkwell in perfect condition, impressed with the name C. CROLIUS/MANUFACTURER/ MANHATTAN WELLS, NEW YORK was excavated in New Orleans.

Potters in Ohio, Kentucky, and western Pennsylvania shipped their wares via barge down the Ohio and Mississippi Rivers. Even today, it's not unusual to find stoneware pieces made by the Eagle Pottery of Greensboro, Pennsylvania, imprinted with the names of Kentucky merchants.

At the same time, potters in Kentucky, Indiana, and Illinois were producing stoneware marked for merchants in Mississippi and Louisiana, particularly New Orleans. Stoneware pieces bearing the imprint of I THOMAS, a Maysville, Kentucky, potter, are found occasionally in New Orleans antique shops.

By the 1850s railroads were beginning to play a role in the distribution of stoneware. Before the end of the century, the boxcar became the standard method of shipping stoneware long distances. The railroads enabled potters in the Midwest to ship their wares to the Great Plains states and to the Pacific Coast. That's why pieces marked by the Macomb Pottery of Macomb, Illinois, the Uhl Pottery of Evansville, Indiana, and the Redway Pottery of Redway, Minnesota, are often seen in California and other western states, including Texas and Arkansas.

REDWARE AND YELLOWWARE

Collectors of stoneware are often confronted with redware and yellowware. While both of these pottery types have their enthusiasts, neither has come close to attaining the popularity of salt-glazed stoneware.

The country's first potters made redware for the kitchen and dairy from the same surface-dug red burning clays they used in the manufacture of bricks and roof tiles. Requiring only the simplest of kilns and equipment, redware was fired at a point between 1,000 and 1,200 degrees centigrade. (Stoneware is fired at nearly 1,300 degrees.) Since it did not fuse or vitrify, the result was a soft, fragile, and somewhat porous product. A flowerpot is a good example.

It was thus essential that redware crocks, jugs, and other pieces be glazed to prevent the contents from seeping through. The glaze commonly used contained a high percentage of lead. When the vessel was used for storing cider, vinegar, pickles, or other acid-containing liquids or foods, the results were scary. Tiny pieces of lead glaze often flaked off the vessel's interior walls and dissolved into whatever was being stored inside. This sometimes caused lead poisoning, which often was fatal.

Redware was produced in the "Dutch" counties of Pennsylvania where the Swiss Mennonites and Germans from the Rhine Palatine settled in the eighteenth century. Their potteries produced fruit pie dishes, apple butter crocks, turk's head cake molds, and other such pieces, none of which ever seemed to have occurred to New England potters.

To dress up their redware, they used white or yellow slip. Manganese oxide produced a brownish black hue for teapots. Copper filings were used to make a green glaze.

Redware was produced in quantity up until around the 1850s. As late as the 1920s, potteries in a handful of rural communities were still making redware for local use. New or old, redware pieces were rarely marked or signed.

Yellowware, produced from yellow clays finer in texture than red clays and lighter in weight than those used in making stoneware, was manufactured in huge quantities from the late 1840s until the mid-1920s. The distinctive yellow clay was found in New Jersey, Pennsylvania, Kentucky, and Ohio. A concentration of potteries around East Liverpool, Ohio, south of Youngstown and close to the Pennsylvania border in the extreme eastern part of the state, is said to have produced as much yellowware as the rest of the nation combined. Potters in East Liverpool were active until the early years of the twentieth century.

Yellowware often consisted of pitchers, bowls, chamber pots, food molds, plates, and serving platters. Each piece was coated with an alkaline or lead glaze that made the natural yellow of the clay much more vivid.

Yellowware was almost always molded, rather than thrown on a wheel. Rarely was a piece marked with a maker's name.

Yellowware was also turned out in England using the same mass-production techniques. It thus can be difficult trying to document the country in which a particular piece was made, much less establish the name of the potter or pottery.

About Glazes

Stoneware can get along without glaze, the thin, smooth coating that makes each piece shiny and seals the surface. The flowerpot is an example. But glaze makes stoneware easier to clean, more attractive in appearance, and more pleasant to handle.

With stoneware, salt glazes, described in the previous chapter, are the most common. During the firing, common table salt was thrown into the kiln. The salt would vaporize and combine with the surface of the clay to produce sodium silicate, the chemical name for salt glaze.

Salt glazing was a less than perfect process, however. Because the pieces were stacked upon one another in the kiln, with the base of one piece resting atop the rim of another, the interior surfaces of many crocks, churns, pitchers, and other wide-mouthed pieces were often poorly glazed. The salt vapor was unable to get into the partially blocked interior

A typical salt-glazed jug from around 1850, the product of J. & E. Norton, Bennington, Vermont.

spaces. And in the case of small-mouthed pieces, the interiors were scarcely glazed at all.

Another failing occurred when the salt was added too early in the firing process, before the surface of the pieces had become fluid enough to react with the vapor. Once the pieces cooled, the glaze powdered and dropped away, leaving the ware dry and unglazed.

SLIP GLAZE

In general, the usual method of applying glaze in pottery making is to dip the pottery, once baked and called "biscuit," into a thin liquid glaze, and then fire it again. By the beginning of the nineteenth century, many American stoneware potters were beginning to use a variation of this glazing method, in addition to salt glazing.

These glazes, called slip or loam glazes, were prepared from natural clays that were strained and mixed with water to produce a creamy mixture, and into which the pieces were dipped. The best known and most popular of the slip glazes was discovered and used by potters in and around Albany, New York, during the first decades of the nineteenth century. It came to be called "Albany slip." The clay used in its production was shipped to all parts of the United States during the final decades of the century. According to Georgeanna Greer, writing in *American Stonewares*, clays of the same type were later mined in large quantities at Elkhart, Indiana, and Rowley, Michigan.

After 1850, it became almost standard practice to brush the interior surface of pieces to be fired with dark brown Albany slip before they were stacked in the kiln. This provided the stable inside surface that was needed. The exterior surface was salt glazed.

Late in the nineteenth century, slip glazes also came to be used on the exterior of stoneware pottery as well as on the interior. In such cases, a piece was partially filled with the slip, which was swirled around until the interior surface was coated. The vessel was then dipped into a slip-filled vat to coat the exterior.

Albany slip glaze produced a dark brown finish.

Slip clay produced a smooth, opaque glaze, often chocolate brown in color. When the firing temperature was extremely high, a reddish brown or mahogany hue could result.

The salt that was added to the kiln and fine wood ash—called fly ash—also affected slip glaze. Salt vapors and the ash sometimes combined to produce patches of yellow or green amidst the dark brown. Direct flames that licked the glaze also bleached the slip and reduced its sheen.

Albany slip glazes and other clays that produced dark brown hues remained popular into the 1900s. Late in the nineteenth century, America was swept by a "hygienic revolution" and white became associated with cleanliness. Dark-color crocks and jugs fell into disfavor. By the time the revolution began to ebb, stoneware itself was being replaced by glassware and modern refrigeration.

ALKALINE GLAZE

In the early years of the nineteenth century, a distinctively different stoneware tradition based upon an alkaline glaze that employed wood ash, clay, and sand developed in an isolated area of South Carolina. The use of this unusual glaze spread rapidly through parts of the southeastern United States.

Alkaline glaze is hard and very durable, shiny and transparent. Its particular color is determined by the amount of iron it contains. Colors can range from cream and tan to olive-green and brown.

Many of the very earliest potters in South Carolina had produced red earthenware, coating it with a lead glaze. But earthenware was fragile and had only limited value when it came to food preservation and storage.

In most areas of the country, particularly the Northeast, salt-glazed stoneware was the alternative. But in rural areas of the South, salt was often in short supply and very costly.

To import Albany-type clay for glaze was also too expensive. Alkaline glaze was a better-than-adequate substitute.

Alkaline-glazed stoneware was first produced in quantity during the early 1800s in what, at the time, was the legislative district of Edgefield, South Carolina (and which is now made up of the Edgefield, Aiken, Saluda, McCormick, and Greenwood counties). Most of the Edgefield potters were concentrated in an area that is now known as Horse Creek Valley in present-day Aiken County. By 1840, according to *Crossroads of Clay*, there were more than two dozen potters operating in Edgefield.

Edgefield potters used local clays and had access to nearby hardwood forests, which produced wood for fuel and for wood ash, the fluxing agent in the production of the alkaline glaze. Water was also available. The ash could be produced from either hard or soft woods. Some potters used hickory or oak; others preferred pine. The clay was often the very same clay that was used in making the pottery itself. The sand was usually the pure fine sand that the potter encountered when digging the clay.

The proper amounts of wood ash, clay, and sand were mixed with water. The mixture was then ground, often in the potter's hand-operated glaze mill. The syrupy mixture was placed into a vat and the pieces to be fired were dipped into it. They had the consistency of belt leather at this stage. In the case of very large objects, such as a churn or water cooler, for example, the glaze was poured over the piece. When the pieces were dry, they were ready for the kiln.

The glaze, called "tobacco spit" or "watermelon glaze" by the potters, was drippy and runny in texture and olive to olive-brown in color. Adding slaked lime to the mix resulted in a smoother glaze surface and modified the color to a lighter yellow-green or gray-green. The color was also determined by the amount of iron present in the clay and glaze ingredients.

One of the principal characteristics of alkaline stoneware

N. Ramey, a South Carolina potter, turned out this three-gallon ovoid jar with its greenish-brown alkaline glaze around 1850.

is that the same glaze appears on both the interior and exterior of every piece. Salt-glazed exteriors are an extreme rarity.

Edgefield potters produced many of the standard stoneware pieces—jars, jugs, pitchers, churns, and pan-form molds. The latter were large mixing bowls with lug handles mounted opposite each other just below the rim. Tall pan-form bowls and bowls with flaring mouths (sometimes called clabber bowls) were used as cream risers. Small bottles, flasks, water coolers, and large vessels for storing water, cider, and wine were also produced.

Much of the stoneware that was turned out at Edgefield was decorated with slip that was brushed on or trailed on before firing. White, off-white, or dark brown, the slip was frequently applied to the bodies of jugs and jars and sometimes to the bases of mixing bowls and cream risers.

Stoneware from the Collin Rhodes pottery bears the maker's mark C. RHODES FACTORY, lettered in trailed slip. Some pieces were decorated with numbers to indicate a vessel's capacity. Two-color floral pieces are seen occasionally. White-slip loops and swags are common to pieces produced at the Trapp-Chandler and Thomas Chandler potteries.

African-American slaves were deeply involved in the production and decoration of Edgefield pottery. Some created unusual face vessels. These often consisted of large jugs onto which facial features were molded in applied clay. A figural bottle in the collection of the Charleston Museum is believed to be the work of an African-American slave potter named Jim Lee, who is said to have worked at the Bodie Factory in the Kirksey's Crossroads area of Edgefield, according to an essay in *Crossroads of Clay*. The bottle is believed to bear the likeness of a local preacher who is garbed in a uniform, complete with buttons and epaulets.

A slave named Dave became recognized as a potter of exceptional skill. He often signed the pieces he created. Huge, heavy, thick-walled storage jars, some of them capable of holding as much as forty gallons, were Dave's specialty. Two or four lug handles were attached to each jar's upper body below the rim. Some of these vessels bear Dave's signature. Others have the letters LM incised on the shoulders, the initials of Lewis Miles, who owned the pottery where the jars were made. Some pieces signed by Dave are dated. The dates range from 1834 to 1860.

As early as 1820, the use of alkaline glaze began to spread, with potters in Georgia, Alabama, Mississippi, and even Texas taking up the technique. A handful of southern potters still produce alkaline-glazed stoneware today, carrying on a tradition established in South Carolina almost two hundred years ago.

BRISTOL GLAZE

Anyone who has visited a flea market of any size or is a veteran yard-sale enthusiast is likely to be aware of the latest form of saltware glaze. Known as Bristol glaze because it is said to have been developed by potters in Bristol, England,

Both Bristol and Albany glazes were used in making this one-quart whiskey jug, which was stamped with an advertisement for its owner.

and dating to the Victorian period, the glaze was used well into the 1920s by American commercial potters. Smooth and opaque white, Bristol glaze was prepared not from raw materials that happened to be available to the potter, but from ceramic chemicals.

Bristol glaze was often used in combination with Albany-type slip glazes to produce the ubiquitous brown-and-white crocks and jugs that are available for purchase about anywhere old things—as opposed to real antiques—are sold. Not only were such vessels machine made, they were machine decorated, too. Small designs were stamped or sprayed onto their outer surfaces.

Stoneware pieces produced in the early decades of the twentieth century have little character. One piece of the same type looks exactly like any other. Even the glazes are all the same, with scarcely any defects. Such pieces are serviceable and durable, but they lack the originality, artistry, tradition, and the beauty of earlier stoneware.

The Art of the Decorator

From the very first, American stoneware was incised, stamped, brushed with slip, and, later, stenciled to give the ware color and dramatic appeal. Decorative styles are almost as varied as the pieces themselves.

It is generally true that stoneware from potteries in the South and Midwest was not as elaborately decorated as the output from New England and New York potters. That's because potteries in the South and Midwest, for the most part, did not come into existence until well into the nineteenth century, when competition was keen. Stoneware had to be produced as quickly and as inexpensively as possible. Ornamentation of any kind was an exception.

In early potteries, it was usually the potter himself who did the decorating. As the industry expanded and specialization began to prevail, men and women began devoting themselves to the pursuit of decoration exclusively. Decorators were sometimes itinerant craftsmen or women who traveled from one pottery to another as their services were needed. This explains why similarly decorated pieces sometimes come from different potteries.

Incising was a decorating technique that involved cutting the outline of a design into soft clay with a thin metal rod or wood-handled instrument that had a sharp blade or tip. In its simplest form, the incised decoration took the form of a band at or near the top of the pot. Such bands were not only decorative, but they aided the potter in positioning the vessel's handles as well.

In much of the early stoneware produced in New England, designs were scratched into the surface with the tip of a nail or the end of a stiff piece of wire. Incising the surface layer of clay often revealed a contrasting color. Called sgraffito, this decorating technique was used from the early nineteenth century until the 1840s.

For incised designs, leaves, flowers, and birds were popular subjects. Large designs, sometimes depicting sailing ships or the American flag, are also seen, but these are rare.

Incised doves adorn this blue-banded water cooler, produced by L. & B. Chace, Massachusetts potters, around 1860.

Incised designs, large as well as small, were frequently highlighted with cobalt blue.

Impressing, another method of decorating, was faster and more mechanical than incising. Impressing involved the use of either a coggle wheel or a hand stamp.

The simplest coggle was a coin that had been notched around the edge with a knife or saw blade. The coin was pierced in the center, and a nail was then inserted in the hole and used as an axis in rolling the coin and forming a decorative band. Toothed gears from clocks were another type of early coggle. More sophisticated coggles took the form of a small wheel with a sunken or incised design. A handle was attached to the center of the wheel with a cotter pin. Decorative banding was done with the coggle. To apply a band, the potter simply held the wheel against the moist clay as he rotated the vessel. Different potters had their own distinctive banding designs.

Hand stamps were made of fired clay or carved out of hard wood. Stamps in the form of crescents, leaves, and even

BOSTON was stamped onto the surface of this multibanded storage jar, produced between 1810 and 1830.

fish were used for decorative designs. They were also used to impress the pot maker's mark into the damp clay. The simplest marks were merely initials. Other times they included the full name of the potter or pottery and the city and state where the pottery was located. Unfortunately, many early potters did not mark their wares. In backwoods areas, there was usually only one potter who supplied the needs of several settlements; in other words, everyone knew who made the pots. There was scarcely any need to sign them.

Late in the nineteenth century, potteries began stamping their pots with the names of merchants who had ordered the vessels. Sometimes novice collectors mistake these names for maker's marks.

Merchants' names were used on jugs more frequently than on any other type of vessel. The jugs were used for the storage of vinegar, cider, wine, and other liquids. Dealers in hard liquor also ordered such jugs.

In West Virginia and western Pennsylvania, from the late 1860s through the early 1900s, potters produced *stenciled stoneware*. While stencils were convenient for the application

A huge (twenty-gallon) and handsomely stenciled storage jar from the Eagle Pottery in Nashville, Tennessee.

of maker's marks or the names of wholesalers, they were also used for creating flowers, fruits, and many different types of geometric patterns.

The Hamilton and Jones Pottery of Greensboro, Pennsylvania, has become especially well known for stenciled pieces. Some of the Greensboro pieces, particularly large crocks and pitchers, feature free-hand brush painting along with stenciled designs, and sometimes brush painting alone.

Stenciling, impressing, and incising were used in applying the capacity mark, a numeral indicating the amount in gallons that could be contained in each vessel. Capacity marks were often encircled with other incised decorations or finished with blue glaze. Sometimes they were incorporated into a larger design.

The most popular decorating technique was the application of *surface-glazed color*. An oxide of cobalt, which produces blue, was the most commonly used. It blended well with stoneware grays and, unlike other oxides, proved remarkably stable in high firing temperatures. And a little bit went a long way, meaning it was economical. Manganese oxide, producing brown, also found use, but only on rare occasions. The same can be said of copper oxide, which produces green.

To prepare cobalt oxide for use, it was mixed with silica and gum arabic. The silica served as a flux that melted in the firing, while the gum arabic was the binder. Water was added to the mixture to form either a paste or a liquid.

The glaze was applied with a stiff brush or a slip cup. Free-hand painting with a brush involved everything from a fast stroke or two around the handles to unusual and elaborate scenes that covered much of the vessel's outer surface.

The slip cup was a small, hand-held container, sometimes with a flask shape, that was originally meant for decorating with slip, a clay solution of creamy consistency. But the slip cup worked just as well with oxide glazes. At the top of the cup there was an opening for filling. There was a second opening in the side into which a quill fitted. Sometimes

Flower and leaf designs were a staple with decorators who wielded slip cups.

the opening in the top held a cork or stopper which was pierced by a quill. In either case, the cup was tilted and the glaze flowed through the quill onto the pot surface, creating a line of color. The thickness of the line depended on the diameter of the quill and the speed with which it was drawn over the surface.

When working with cobalt oxide, flowers and leaf designs were standard forms of decoration. Birds were common, too. They included pigeons, chickens, sparrows, robins, peacocks, and a variety of game birds. But often the species is not identifiable; the bird can combine the features of several different species.

Among animal designs, deer were the most popular. Oddly, deer were sometimes drawn with zebra stripes. Rabbits appeared in a variety of poses. Crocks made by the Nortons of Bennington sometimes featured lions. A wide variety of fish appeared on early stoneware. Some potters applied their fish designs with a hand stamp, then glazed them blue.

Patriotic designs, usually inspired by the War of 1812, led

to the use of eagles and the American flag in stoneware design. Naval scenes became popular as well, although these pieces are relatively rare today.

Some designs are highly inventive, representing figures or scenes out of the decorator's experience or imagination. For example, a jug from the Fulper pottery in Flemington, New Jersey, produced around 1890, features a pair of performing acrobats. (It brought $28,600 at a Sotheby's auction in 1986.) A five-gallon churn from the Hart pottery in Fulton, New York, offers a head and shoulder portrait of a scruffy man smoking a pipe. (It fetched $19,000 at a Denlinger auction.) A three-gallon Bennington crock portraying a preening rooster perched on a fence, with a house and pine trees in the background, opened at $3,000. After several minutes of very active bidding, it sold for $12,000.

Once in a while, decoration was meant to represent the use the piece was to have. For example, a Connecticut collector owns a two-gallon jug that pictures a large tomato with its stem and several leaves attached. Impressed near the neck, where the maker's mark would ordinarily be found, are the words FRESH TOMATOES. Since the mouth of the jug is only 1¾ inches wide, the vessel could hardly have been used for the storage of tomatoes themselves. Perhaps it was meant for storing tomato juice or puree.

During the latter half of the nineteenth century, an ever-increasing number of potters, and the increased competition that resulted, forced potters to employ mass-production methods. The day of elaborate decoration waned as a result. Such designs as eagles, flags, sailing ships, human figures and faces, and exotic animals gave way to simple birds and flowers. Later, a few swirls created by dipping a brush in cobalt blue was made to suffice.

Types of Stoneware

Jugs, jars, crocks, and churns were the standard pieces offered by every nineteenth-century stoneware potter. Manufactured in huge quantities, they sold at prices that seem unreal in today's marketplace. For instance, in the 1850s, the Albany Stoneware Factory in New York sold decorated three-gallon jugs for $6 *per dozen*. And in the 1860s, one could buy five-gallon decorated butter churns from E. & L. P. Norton in Bennington, Vermont, for $13 a dozen. Many potteries also produced an array of more specialized items, including bowls, pitchers, cuspidors, and chamber pots.

While each of the standard vessels had a basic form, countless variations of each were produced. Following are the most frequently seen types of vessels.

JUGS, CROCKS, AND JARS

Jugs

Of all the many types of stoneware, the jug is the most common. A tall, rounded vessel with a narrow neck meant to be stopped with a cork or wooden plug, the jug ranged in size from one-half gallon to six gallons, although jugs with eight- and ten-gallon capacities are seen occasionally. All true jugs have handles. Most have merely a single handle, but those that are four gallons or larger are often double-handled.

Jugs were used for water, liquor, wine, vinegar, cider, and oil. Sometimes the mouth of a jug would include a pouring spout. This was called a syrup jug.

During the early years of the nineteenth century, jugs were more ovoid, that is, they tended to be full-bodied, with the middle of the jug greater in girth than the top or base. They could be bell-shaped, too, with the lower portion being the widest part. Around mid-century, sides became straighter and shoulders began to form. Before the century ended, jugs were cylindrical in shape.

Early jugs, such as this two-gallon example from the BENNINGTON Factory, tended to be ovoid in form.

Most jugs had free-standing handles called strap handles, which were attached vertically in pairs. Each strap handle was formed by pulling a piece of clay into a strip and cutting it to the desired length. What was to be the upper end of the handle was fixed to the pot first, and then the clay strip would be smoothed, lengthened, properly looped, and attached at the bottom. Strap handles could be either flat or rounded. Some had grooves into which the fingers fit when lifting.

Jugs almost always have lug handles. Lids are much less common.

Crocks

Another extremely popular stoneware form, the crock is a tall, rounded, and wide-mouthed vessel that was used for storing butter, lard, salted meat, and many other foods. Crocks were also used in processing and storing pickled foods, such as cucumbers.

As in the case of jugs, early crocks were ovoid, with greater girth in the middle than at the base or top. By the 1850s, crocks had become straight-sided. Most crocks had fitted wood or ceramic lids. On some, there is a lid ledge inside the crock mouth upon which the lid rested.

By the 1850s, crocks were generally straight-sided. This one-gallon example was produced by E. & L. P. Norton of Bennington, Vermont.

Crocks were fitted with handles which were mounted in pairs on opposite sides of the vessel. Called lug handles, they were made of short strips of flat or rounded clay which was bent into an inverted U shape, then attached along the crock's entire length to the crock walls at a point two or three inches below the rim. In early crocks, the upper portion of the handle was sometimes bent outward from the crock side to create an open loop. The fingertips could then be inserted into the loop when lifting.

In both crocks and jugs, the handles represent the weakest part of the structure. Thus, when examining a piece, never lift it by the handles. There's always a chance of one snapping or cracking. Instead, take a firm grasp of the vessel at the sides.

Jars

Like crocks, jars are wide-mouthed containers, but they're slimmer. They, too, were used for preserving and storing foods. Some had lug handles; others did not.

Some early jars are slightly ovoid in shape, but jars are usually straight-sided with the neck slightly smaller in diameter than the body and base. Jars were made in sizes from one gallon to five gallons. They were almost always fitted with lug handles.

By the mid-nineteenth century, potters were turning out ceramic lids for their jars. Lid ledges within the jar mouth became common.

Jars were used for storing meat preserved in salt, for butter and lard, soft soap, pickles, cream, and apple butter and other fruit butters. And there also were cookie jars, of course.

Jars of a gallon or more in size were fitted with lug handles, although strap handles were not uncommon. And there are examples of very large jars which were fitted with not two, but four handles.

CHURNS AND BATTER JUGS

Churns

Usually tall, cylinder-shaped, and topped with a simple neck or collar, stoneware churns were not produced until the nineteenth century. Before that time, milk or cream was churned in earthenware vessels or ones made of staved wood.

Churns are tall and cylinder-shaped. This first-rate example dates to about 1870.

In churning, milk or butter or cream is agitated by a kind of plunger called a dasher. The dasher is a wooden pole the size of a broomstick, one end of which is fitted with crossed wooden slats or a flat disk with holes drilled through it. Stoneware churns withstood the vigorous up-and-down action of the dasher better than earthenware or wood. And stoneware churns were much easier to clean.

Churns were made in two-, three-, four-, five-, six-, eight-, ten-, and twelve-gallon sizes. They were fitted with wood or ceramic lids. The lid had a central hole to accommodate the handle of the dasher. Lug handles were typical.

Batter Jugs

Rather like a pitcher in use and a pail in form, the batter jug was a slightly ovoid, wide-mouthed vessel with a tubular pouring spout. It was used to mix and pour pancake batter. The usual sizes are three-quarter gallon, one gallon, or one and one-half gallon.

The batter jug was often fitted with a stoneware lid or tin lid manufactured by a local tinsmith. Occasionally a second lid was provided to fit the spout.

Batter jugs have heavy spouts and a lug handle to aid in pouring.

Early batter jugs had heavy handles at the sides, which could be gripped easily. Later jugs were fitted with a bail handle, similar to the semicircular handle common to a kettle or a pail. Fitted with a wooden grip at the center, the handle was attached to either side of the mouth. Often an additional cupped handle, similar in shape to the "ears" of a straight-sided crock, was applied to the jug's base opposite the spout. This served as an aid in pouring.

Batter jugs were often decorated with light dabs of cobalt at the handle bases and around the spout. Sometimes decorators applied small floral designs beneath the spout and on the back. Anything more elaborate than this represents a real find today.

Don't expect batter jugs to be anywhere near as common as crocks or jugs. While a nineteenth-century household needed a good storage of vessels, a family could get along quite nicely with only one batter jug.

FIGURALS

Stoneware vessels that take the form of an animal, a human, or some inanimate object represent yet another specialty. Such figurals, formed in molds, have been traced as far back as ancient Egypt.

Some of the best of the earliest American stoneware figurals were produced at Bennington, Vermont, in the mid-1800s. As early as 1841, Julius Norton was advertising the availability of ink stands that were topped with the figure of a greyhound. Lavishly decorated with blue, these creations were unabashed copies of an earlier English piece.

Daniel Greatbach, an English potter who worked in Bennington, produced stoneware whiskey bottles that took the form of a coachman. One example is dated 1849. Greatback also turned out the coachman in glazed and brown mottled earthenware, that is, Rockingham ware.

Pennsylvania potters produced quaint figurals called

"blow birds." They were children's whistles. Dabbed lightly with cobalt and salt-glazed, they usually were made in the shape of roosters, robins, barnyard animals, and, occasionally, human figures. All were hollow. The user blew into an opening in the beak or tail of the blow bird to produce a high-pitched sound that emanated from a vent in the back or bottom of the object.

Dogs with long, thick, and frizzy hair—poodles, apparently—are another popular figural. English potters at Staffordshire produced such pieces in white earthenware and Rockingham ware during the 1700s, and the form was copied by American potters in Ohio, Pennsylvania, and New York. They were used as doorstops, banks, whistles, and mantelpieces.

A variation, a reclining lion on an oval pedestal, has been attributed to the Clark and Company pottery in Lyons, New York. The lion can have one of several different patterns of stripes on its back, but all have blue eyes.

During the second half of the nineteenth century, most American figurals were produced in the South and Midwest. Potters in Georgia and the Carolinas created brown glazed whiskey jugs that took the form of grotesque human heads.

The Anna Pottery Company produced a variety of pig flasks saluting Midwest railroads.

In Illinois, the Anna Pottery Co. produced a wide variety of these pieces. In fact, the Anna Pottery Co., which was operated by the Kirkpatrick family, is sometimes called the leading American kiln when it comes to figurals. Pigs and other barnyard animals were among those produced. One variation of the famous Anna pig was decorated with an incised map of Western railroads as they existed in 1889. The piece was presented to railway workers and customers. A whiskey jug adorned with molded snakes was another specialty of the Anna pottery. These vessels were often intended as presentation pieces and sometimes carried uncomplimentary remarks concerning the recipient's drinking habits.

MISCELLANEOUS

Pitchers

Pitchers are most common in one-quart, one-half-gallon, one-and-one-half-gallon, and two-gallon sizes. Three-gallon

In baluster-shaped pitchers, the vessel's collar represents as much as a third of the piece's height. This example, German in origin, dates to the very early nineteenth century.

pitchers, used in farm homes for storing milk, are seen occasionally.

Most pitchers have a bulbous body that tapers into a cylindrical neck and collar. The collar usually represents about one-third of the vessel's height. There are also straight-sided pitchers, but they are rare. Pitcher handles are always strap handles.

Bottles and Flasks

Produced in great quantity and variety during the nineteenth century, bottles and flasks were widely used because they kept liquids cool before refrigeration was common. They commonly held beer or soft drinks, such as sarsaparilla.

Bottles were turned out in a variety of cylindrical shapes until the 1850s. From that time on, they were made with straight sides and a cone-shaped neck that tapered to a heavy lip. This allowed wire to be tightly tied beneath the lip to hold the cork in place. They were also usually made in one-quart sizes, although one-pint bottles are common, too.

This one-pint ale bottle, finished in Bristol glaze, dates to the 1880s.

Only a relatively few bottles and flasks are decorated. What they do have, however, are imprints bearing the name of the brewer, bottler, tavern, or storekeeper who purchased the piece.

Bowls

Deep round dishes used for holding liquids or foods were very popular in the middle Atlantic states but scarcely manufactured at all in some other areas. Before 1860 or so, bowls were made with sloping sides. Some were deep; others shallow. They were often called pans, not bowls. Such vessels were one, one and one half, and two gallons in size.

Bowls manufactured in the later decades of the nineteenth century have a more classic shape, which includes a heavily banded rim. Deep bowls of one- or two-gallon capacity, with a pair of lug handles and a pouring spout, were often used in separating cream from milk. They were called milk bowls or milk crocks. Handsomely decorated bowls, also with lug handles, were used as serving bowls.

Mugs

Manufactured in one-half-pint and one-pint sizes, mugs were usually cylinder-shaped and, aside from banding or combing, were not elaborately decorated.

Chamber Pots

In 1977, a group of archeologists working near Chestnut Street in Philadelphia found good-sized fragments of four salt-glazed stoneware chamber pots bearing the A D stamp of Anthony Duche, who operated a pottery in that city from 1730 to 1740. About the same time, other archeologists found a complete chamber pot with the same A D mark in a privy at 8 South Front Street. At the time, these were believed to be the earliest examples of marked American glazed stoneware to be found in the northeastern United States.

Chamber pots were short, wide, and slightly globular in

form, with broad flattened rims. Each was fitted with a stout strap handle. Two sizes, adult and child, were manufactured.

Colanders

Used for draining or straining a variety of foods, colanders usually took the form of perforated bowls, although there were some that resembled wide-mouthed jars. They were made as ordinary jars or bowls, then pierced by the potter before the clay dried.

Ring Jugs

Also called a ring flask or ring bottle, the ring jug takes the form of a circular tube with a round spout at the top. It was meant to be carried around a person's upper arm. Some have a flat base which enables the piece to stand upright. Manufactured beginning late in the nineteenth century, ring jugs usually have a capacity of three-fourths of a quart or one quart.

Ring jugs are sometimes called "haymakers' bottles." It's said that they were frequently used by men who worked in the fields, cutting hay and spreading it out to dry. But such a tale has to be regarded as fiction to anyone familiar with a scythe and the way in which the implement was used. A ring bottle would have been an encumbrance. It's also said the ring jug was intended to be carried by a man making a long ride on horseback. He could refresh himself from such a bottle without having to dismount.

Cuspidors

In Ulysses S. Grant's home in Galena, Illinois, built and furnished for him after the Civil War by grateful hometown citizens, there was at least one cuspidor (known as spittoons then) in every room, with the exception of his daughter Nellie's bedroom. Bowl-shaped and with a large flared lip, the cuspidor was usually the product of larger potteries. Not only were they made of classic stoneware with blue decoration, but they were also available in glazed redware and the glazed brown-and-yellow mottled earthenware known as Rockingham ware.

Flowerpots

Flowerpots were flat-bottomed with slightly flared sidewells and with a central drainage hole in the bottom. They were produced both glazed and unglazed. Some had saucers attached.

Occasionally flowerpots were decorated with a small floral spray, and these are the examples sought by collectors. Ballard and F. Woodworth, both Burlington, Vermont, potters, are among those who produced flowerpots of high quality and imprinted their output with their names.

A Ballard price list, dated April 12, 1875, and reprinted in the *Stoneware Collector's Journal*, offers "earthen flower pots of every description" that ranged in size from one-eighth gallon to one full gallon. Starter pots for seedlings, called greenhouse pots, classified in inches, were available in nine different sizes from two and one-half inches to ten inches. Saucers for the pots, from four inches to ten inches in size, could be purchased, too.

The price list featured "ornamental hanging vases," a Ballard specialty, for which he had obtained a government patent. Produced as either ornamental or plain, the vases came in three sizes—one-eighth, one-fourth, and one-half gallon. A dozen ornamental hanging vases could be purchased for $5. Ballard also sold the chains to hang the vases, at $3 a dozen.

Water Coolers

These large cylinder-shaped vessels usually date to the final decades of the nineteenth century. They were fitted with a small neck that could easily be corked, a pair of heavy strap handles, and an opening for a spigot near the base.

Rouletted, cobalt-decorated, and hand-incised, this handsome water cooler, attributed to the Wingender pottery in Haddonfield, New Jersey, was produced around 1885.

Because of the enormous quantity of stoneware pieces produced during the nineteenth century, examples of almost every type are still available to the collector. They can be purchased in an enormous range of shapes and sizes, with all manner of decoration, and at prices to suit every budget.

Imported Stoneware

While American stoneware potteries did a thriving business during the second half of the nineteenth century, stoneware containers were also imported. For the most part, there were bottles, jars, jugs, and other vessels that contained foreign products in demand in America. Collectors of American stoneware generally shun foreign wares, but they are frequently offered for sale at flea markets and antique shows. It makes sense to be knowledgeable about them, otherwise mistakes can be made.

BRITAIN, GERMANY, AND FRANCE

Most of the stoneware imports of the nineteenth century were British. The earliest vessels to make the Atlantic crossing were often straight-sided, salt-glazed bottles for beer, ale, and ginger beer. Eight ounces was the standard size. Dark brown was the standard color.

Late in the nineteenth century, the typical salt-glazed bottle was supplanted by one in which the upper half had a dark, Albany-type slip, while the lower half was much lighter in color and smoother. In other words, the typical British bottle, jar, or jug is brown and white.

Ink was another very popular British import, and ink containers were, like early bottles, covered in a brown glaze. There were small ink containers for individuals and larger, straight-sided ones for commercial use. These had a capacity of about one pint and sometimes were fitted with a pouring spout. Such containers were also used for stove blacking and other polishes.

During the latter half of the nineteenth century, large, wide-mouthed ovoid vessels with heavy, paired handles were imported from Great Britain. These contained no product; they were meant for sale as storage vessels. Large jugs with loop handles were also imported during this period and used for storage. Both forms were finished with glistening brown slip glaze.

The most frequently seen German stoneware vessels take the form of tall, often cylinder-shaped, jugs, salt-glazed on the exterior, which were used as containers for mineral water, distilled liquor, and cordials. Many of these pieces have the impressed marks of Rhenish or Dutch beverage manufacturers. The colors can be gray-white, tan, or light brown, depending upon the iron content of the clay.

It is not difficult to confuse some of the traditional German forms with American pieces of the same period. For example, German potters produced a wide-mouthed jar, slightly ovoid in shape, with paired open loop handles. More than a few of these were decorated with blue-cobalt. How does one distinguish these from American stoneware? One tipoff is the clay, which can be very white. Another clue is that German decorators were more meticulous than their American counterparts, many of whom seemed to have been in a bit of a rush when applying the slip. German potters were also more likely to use incised decorations, filling the designs with cobalt.

Stoneware from France is much less common. "I have seen more of this ware unearthed in New Orleans than any other American city," says Georgeanna H. Greer in *American Stonewares*. Ms. Greer also recalled seeing French imported stoneware in Savannah, Georgia, and Charlestown, South Carolina.

Like British stoneware, much of that from France takes the form of bottles. These were used for inks and oils. Many are straight-sided, but some tend to be ovoid with two or more rings about the neck or just below the shoulder. In size, they vary from about one-half pint to one quart. The colors range from light to deep gray.

CHINA

Stoneware was also imported from China, particularly in the years following the great influx of Chinese immigrants during the final decades of the nineteenth century. The newcomers often retained their native preferences in food, which made it necessary to import a variety of foods and seasonings from the homeland.

Soy sauce was one. Squat soy sauce jars, usually about one quart in size, are dark brown and shiny. The main portion vaguely resembles a New England beanpot in shape. Soy sauce jars were perhaps the most common stoneware container to be exported to America from China. These vessels have a jug-type opening at the top and a small pouring spout in the shoulder. Such containers are most likely to be found in cities that were thickly settled with Chinese immigrants. Large soy jars, up to one gallon in size and generally with the same ovoid shape, are encountered in Pacific Coast cities.

Also imported were containers for different types of Asian pickles and preserves.

Ginger, preserved in heavy syrup, was another product Chinese immigrants imported in great quantity. Ginger jars, described by Georgeanna Greer as having a "transparent or white feldspathic glaze and blue decoration underneath the glaze," have been found in most major nineteenth-century port cities. "I have seen them in all of our early southern port cities," says Ms. Greer in *American Stonewares*, "and have purchased them in inland cities as well."

Alcoholic beverages were also imported from China in stoneware containers. While these are called bottles, they are not bottlelike in shape, being bulbous and tapering up to a narrow neck with a flared mouth ring. They are covered in a thick, brownish black glaze.

No matter what size or shape they take, Asian stoneware pieces that were exported to America do not have handles. Any handle that does appear takes the form of a very small loop near the top of the vessel into which a cord was inserted. The cord was not only helpful in handling the vessel, but it could also be used in securing the lid to the piece so it wouldn't get lost.

Asian stoneware of the late nineteenth century is usually quite different in form and size than American stoneware. The two forms are not difficult to tell apart. But many European stoneware pieces, since they often feature glazes that are not unlike their American counterparts, can cause confusion. Keep in mind that the major differences occur in form and decoration.

Buying and Selling

WHAT TO LOOK FOR WHEN BUYING

According to dealers and collectors, the first rule for buying antique stoneware is simple: Buy the best pieces you can afford.

The second rule is to do your homework. Read everything you can about stoneware. Seek out and study stoneware collections at museums and historical societies. Attend stoneware auctions, visit antique shows and shops, and browse local flea markets to familiarize yourself with pieces and prices. Try to latch onto a knowledgeable collector and watch the way in which he or she operates. "Don't come into the field for money," warns Betty Schatzberg. "But," she adds, "if you buy what's unique, and it's the best of its kind, you won't have to worry financially."

In the marketplace of the 1990s, the quality of a piece and

the originality and extravagance of the decoration are the foremost factors in determining value. The form of the piece, whether it's a jug, a crock, or a churn, its size, its age, and even the name of the potter are usually secondary factors. "Always look for a piece that's different," says one dealer.

While you should be seeking an original piece of art, the design shouldn't be too folksy looking. A carefully executed peacock has more value than one that's unsophisticated or exhibits slapdash qualities. "You want the design to be well done," says Betty Schatzberg. "I've seen what is supposed to be a rabbit or a lion, and you have to kind of scratch your head and wonder if that's what it really is. If someone has to tell you what kind of an animal it is, you probably don't want the piece." She further goes on to say, "I like pieces that are artistically done, pieces that are interesting. But you don't want a picture. You're looking for a piece with personality."

Not long ago, the Schatzbergs bought a four-gallon straight-sided crock made by T. H. Harrington, a Lyons, New York, potter. The piece was decorated with a lion. But this was no ordinary lion. It is a bold and confident lion, a real king-of-the-beasts lion, pictured with his head turned, looking behind him. Of the decorator, Joel Schatzberg says, "This guy was an *artist*." The blue in which the lion was executed is bright and dense. The Schatzbergs estimate the piece to be worth $30,000 to $40,000. It was one of sixteen pieces found in an old mill in Newark, New York. The Schatzbergs bought eight of them from the mill owner. "We ended up paying him more for the stoneware than he paid for the mill," Joel Schatzberg says.

Birds and animals are much sought after by collectors, but not all birds and animals. Take deer, for instance. "Deer pieces have really dropped," says Joel Schatzberg. "While a few years ago [1989], you could buy a deer for $5,000 or $6,000, and have felt good about it, now you have to pay only $3,000 or $4,000. People have to realize that deer once were production items. Every pottery had a decorator who made deer, or they borrowed an artist who could turn them out. Now, everybody who wanted a deer has one. The demand has been satisfied."

According to Schatzberg, the pieces that are in the biggest demand are those displaying unusual animals, such as giraffes or llamas. Schatzberg says, "A lot of western New York state potteries did lions, but few were realistic. It makes you wonder how the decorators formed their images. They had to be from memory, an impression that was made after a visit to a zoo or a circus or something."

Dated pieces of stoneware are rare. So are pieces bearing the images of human figures or faces, houses or other buildings, masonic or other fraternal emblems, flags, eagles, shields, and other patriotic symbols, and fish, exotic animals, and sailing ships. Expect to pay premium prices for them.

Many stoneware collectors develop their own specialties. A Connecticut collector buys only pieces representing the output of early Hartford potteries. A New York City collector is seeking one piece for every New York state potter. "Some people collect by names," says Betty Schatzberg. "There is a couple named Boynton, for instance, that collects pieces from Boynton potteries." Still other people collect by type, seeking only butter churns or pitchers. And others want only pieces that depict certain animals such as deer, peacocks, cats, or dogs.

As in any field of collecting, the matter of condition is all-important. What about cracks, a somewhat common flaw? A piece may have a hairline crack—called a "line"—or a deeper, wider, more serious crack, one that can catch a fingernail when you draw it over the surface. Naturally, the bigger the crack, the more the piece is devalued. But the location of the crack is just as critical as the size. If the crack cuts through the decoration, ruining the appearance of the piece, it can diminish the value by as much as 40 or 50 percent, even more. But a line on the back or at the base of a crock or jug, where it's scarcely noticed, may reduce the value by only

10 percent or so. Blistering or flaking that occurred during firing, or base chips or rim chips that resulted from careless use, can also lessen the value of a piece. Again, what's important is whether these imperfections mar the decoration considerably.

During the 1980s, when stoneware prices began to take off, the field attracted counterfeiters. They could produce a high-priced fake by taking an inexpensive, undecorated crock or jug, adding some blue to it, and then refiring it. They could then sell what might have been a $30 or $40 piece for many hundreds, or even many thousands, of dollars.

One way dealers have learned to spot such fakes is by examining the inside walls of a piece. If it was refired, the brown slip coating on the interior will be blistered and no longer smooth. When buying an expensive piece, therefore, it's a good idea to close your eyes and feel it. "Your eyes can lie to you," says Joel Schatzberg. "But with your fingers, you can sometimes feel variations in the surface materials that can tipoff that a piece has been tampered with."

If you have any doubt of the authenticity of a piece, says Schatzberg, take a key or a coin out of your pocket and ask the seller whether you can scratch the surface. "If he says no, don't buy the piece. If it's an authentic salt-glazed piece, you can't scratch it, not even with the point of a knife. Practically nothing can penetrate the surface. But if the item has been tampered with, you can probably carve your initials in it."

In an effort to spot fakes, some collectors use ultraviolet light. When a crock or jug or other piece that has been repaired or reglazed is subjected to ultraviolet radiation, the tampered-with area produces a greenish glow. "Unless you really trust the person you're buying from," says one dealer, "you should subject anything valued at over $3,000 or $4,000 to ultraviolet light."

The test, however, doesn't work *every* time. "During the mid-1980s, restorers got smart," says Barbara Cann, who once sold ultraviolet lights to collectors and dealers. "They started using glaze materials that didn't react to the ultraviolet rays." But most experts feel that ultraviolet light is reliable around 90 percent of the time in exposing fakery.

BUYING FROM DEALERS AND AUCTIONS

One way to avoid getting burned is to buy from a reputable dealer. You're almost certain to have the option of being able to return any piece you find unsatisfactory. Another advantage in buying from a dealer is that you'll be offered only those pieces in which you specialize and in the price range you've designated.

For any item you purchase, also ask for a bill of sale. Be sure it includes the date, a description of the piece (including any defects), the amount paid, and any other conditions of sale. You'll want the bill of sale for your own records as well as for insurance and resale purposes.

Of course, buying at auction is more exciting than buying from a dealer. You may be able to get a piece at a bargain price. This is particularly true toward the auction's end, when prices tend to dip. But real bargains are a rarity nowadays. Remember, at an auction you're not only competing with other collectors but with knowledgeable dealers as well.

Be sure to carefully examine each piece before the auction sale begins. Don't trust the catalog description or the comments of other collectors. Determine the size, origin, age, and condition of each piece in which you're interested.

Once the sale starts, be careful not to let yourself get carried away by the bidding. "Auction fever" can send prices through the roof. Do what dealers do. They set a limit for each piece in which they're interested, and if the bidding goes higher, they bow out.

There's no margin for error when buying at an auction, no opportunity to return a piece with which you are dissatisfied.

"All items are sold as is," say auction catalogues. "All sales are final. No returns."

The only exception to this might concern identification. If you discover that a piece that you've purchased was misidentified by the auction house, and you establish the name of the actual pottery within thirty days following the sale, you can probably get your purchase price refunded. (Be advised that the term "attributed to" does not imply a certified designation of authenticity.) Regarding the matter of size, markings and decoration, defects, physical condition, color, date of manufacture, importance, provenance, and historical relevance, however, all pieces are sold as is.

Notable stoneware auctions are held in the spring and fall by Marlin G. Denlinger (RR 3, Box 3775, Morrisville, VT, 05661) and each spring by Wayne Arthur (RR 2, Box 155, Hughesville, PA, 17737).

BUYING AT FLEA MARKETS

Flea markets are another source of stoneware. They've become big business and they're getting bigger all the time. Take Brimfield, for instance. It's a super flea, attracting more than 3,000 dealers who set up in twenty-two connecting fields stretched out along several miles of Route 20 in south central Massachusetts. As many as 30,000 shoppers turn out. For most of them, Brimfield is serious business. They line up two hours before the biggest lots open, and when the gates part, they storm in. Some dealers operate with walkie-talkies, informing partners of their finds. Brimfield operates for five consecutive days early in May and July and during the second week in September.

Other super fleas include:

Fort Lauderdale Swap Shop, 3291 West Sunrise Blvd., Fort Lauderdale, Florida. Open 365 days a year.

Renniger's Antique and Collectible Outdoor Extravaganza, 740 Noble St., Kutztown, Pennsylvania. Open the last Friday, Saturday, and Sunday weekend of April, June, and September.

Kane County Flea Market, fairgrounds, St. Charles, Illinois. Held the first Sunday of every month and the preceding Saturday.

San Jose Flea Market, 1200 Berryessa Rd., San Jose, California. Open every Wednesday through Sunday.

There are at least two basic strategies as to the best time to go to flea markets. Most dealers and serious collectors get there very early. How early? Bring a flashlight. The theory is that everything that is worthwhile is going to go in the first twenty minutes.

Other collectors ignore the clock. They simply arrive at a time that's convenient for them and shop at their leisure. "There are plenty of treasures the early birds leave behind," says one collector.

Flea market dealers are usually prepared to negotiate somewhat, since as a rule pieces are marked a bit higher than what the dealer expects to get. In bargaining, ask, "Can you do a little better on that?" or "What's your best price?" If you find a piece you like and the price is right, don't procrastinate; buy it on the spot. If it's a real bargain and you hesitate, someone else is sure to snap it up.

You can also comb local flea markets in search of stoneware. "Every now and then a sleeper turns up," says Brad Maxwell, a Dedham, Massachusetts, dealer. "Someone has been cleaning out an attic and is selling what has been found, and they don't know anything about antique stoneware."

Maxwell discourages the idea of buying at roadside antique shops. "What they usually have," he says, "is low-end pieces with high prices." As for yard sales, they're a waste of time, according to Maxwell. Other dealers agree that the average householder offers mostly junk and damaged pieces.

RECORD KEEPING AND STORAGE

Once you've purchased a piece and added it to your collection, make a record of it. This record should include the information on the bill of sale, plus any identification number you want to assign to the piece. Many collectors simply number in sequence the pieces they acquire. When you sell a piece, add the name of the buyer, the date of the transaction, and the amount you received to the record.

It's also a good idea to photograph each piece. Such photos are helpful when acquiring insurance. They also can be invaluable should a piece be stolen and you seek the help of the police in attempting to recover it. If you own valuable pieces, you should definitely insure them against accidental breakage and theft. Such insurance may be included in a homeowner's policy or you may have to provide it through separate coverage. Talk to your insurance agent.

If you have expensive pieces you wish to keep at home, store them inside a locked cabinet. You may wish to install an alarm system in the cabinet. When you plan to be away for an extended period, store the collection in a safer place.

One big plus factor about stoneware is that it's very durable. It doesn't require the special treatment you have to give old prints or phonograph records or some other collectibles. But accidents can occur. For example, don't try displaying a stoneware jug or crock atop a stereo speaker. If it should happen to have a hairline crack, the speaker vibrations could cause the piece to split apart.

SELLING AT AUCTIONS AND TO DEALERS

When it comes to selling stoneware, you can go to either an auction house or a dealer. In the case of an auction, realize that bidders can surprise you. You might be lucky and get a bigger-than-expected price through competitive bidding. On the other hand, the mood of the crowd can swing in the opposite direction and depress the bidding. You can even end up getting less than you paid for the piece.

Look for an auctioneer who has a big following in the stoneware field. The more collectors and dealers the auctioneer can bring together, the more likely you are to benefit.

It's standard practice for the auctioneer to take a percentage commission on each item consigned. Marlin G. Denlinger, whose stoneware auctions in Bennington, Vermont, each April and October are well known to collectors and dealers throughout the country, charges sellers a ten percent commission. Other auctioneers sometimes ask for a smaller percentage, especially in the case of expensive pieces of $5,000 or more. "What's important is not the amount of the commission," says Denlinger. "It's whether your piece is going to be offered to a large and enthusiastic group of prospective buyers. In other words, how much are you going to *net*?"

Ask the auctioneer whether you can establish a base price—a minimum amount you will accept as a bid. If the auctioneer agrees to this, the agreement should be confirmed in writing. There are no base prices at the Bennington auctions, however. "I'm strictly against them," says Marlin Denlinger. "An auction is an auction. A base price is the owner's opinion of what a piece is worth. It has nothing to do with market value. It's not fair to the buyer."

One disadvantage of selling through an auction house is that you have to wait until the auction is scheduled and the sale consummated before you are paid. With a dealer, it's quick. You can have a check in a matter of minutes.

In bargaining with a dealer, keep in mind that he or she will be seeking to buy at wholesale in order to be able to sell at retail. This means that a dealer probably won't offer you much more than half of what you paid for any given piece (providing there has been no great change in market conditions). Don't hesitate to consult more than one dealer, getting prices from each before you make a decision.

If you're seeking to sell several pieces, the dealer may want to take only the best ones. You should set an "all-or-nothing" policy, unless you think you'll be able to sell the lower-end pieces elsewhere.

In the case of low-end items, consider selling at a flea market. This involves renting table space for a day or two and acting as your own dealer. Most newspapers in the antiques field have classified advertising sections in which pieces can be offered for sale.

What's really important in selling is the first rule set down in this chapter. As Brad Maxwell expresses it, "A good piece you can always sell, no matter what you paid for it."

American Stoneware Listings

How to Use This Book

The prices listed in this section refer to the retail value of stoneware pieces, the amount a collector might expect to pay when buying from a dealer, at an auction sale, antique show, or a flea market. In some cases, the prices represent the actual knockdown price at a recent auction (A); in other cases, they are dealer estimates (D).

The listings are arranged alphabetically by type. Descriptive information is as complete as possible, including the potter's name or actual imprint whenever either is available.

Descriptive information also includes judgments as to the quality and condition of each piece. Both, of course, are critical factors in establishing value.

Photographs are often used to illustrate a particular item. Be aware that many imperfections—cracks, chips, and repairs—are often not revealed by a photograph. Photographs are only meaningful when considered in combination with written descriptions.

Quality refers to the degree of excellence of a piece. There are four classifications:

Superior Quality: An item that is at the very top of its class, first-rate in form, design, and execution; a very rare piece.

Excellent Quality: Well above average in terms of form, design, and execution.

Very Good Quality: A piece that is seen with some frequency but is above average in terms of artistic value; a desirable item.

Good Quality: A worthwhile item but one that is seen quite frequently and does not exhibit any outstanding characteristics in terms of design or execution.

Condition refers to the physical state of a piece. The four classifications are as follows:

Fine Condition: The piece is as close as possible to its original state.

Excellent Condition: Above average; no significant flaws, no repairs.

Good Condition: Perhaps a tight hairline crack or two or other minor flaw, but no serious chipping or flaking. No significant damage.

Poor Condition: Although still salable because of one or more outstanding features, this is a piece with a serious fault: a major crack, a missing handle or other part, or obvious repairs or restoration work.

Batter Jugs

One gallon F. H. Cowden Harrisburg, PA
Ovoid in form with large pouring spout and lug handle at base. Impressed with potter's imprint. Attractive stenciled decoration. Bail handle missing, as is one of the "ears" to which handle attaches. (ARTHUR AUCTIONEERING)
Excellent Quality/Good Condition *$200 (A)*

(Capacity Unknown) White's Binghamton, NY
Wide-mouthed spout and lug handle at base. Strokes of blue near opposing loops to which (missing) bail handle attached. Impressed with maker's mark. Hairline cracks at back and top. (COLLECTION OF BILL SULLIVAN)
Good Quality/Good Condition *$225 (A)*

One and one-half gallon Cowden & Wilcox Harrisburg, PA
Ovoid in shape with large pouring spout, lug handle at base, and wire bail handle. Cobalt blue floral decorations on both sides. Dabbed with blue at spout and "ears." Replaced ear. (ARTHUR AUCTIONEERING)
Excellent Quality/Very Good Condition *$475 (A)*

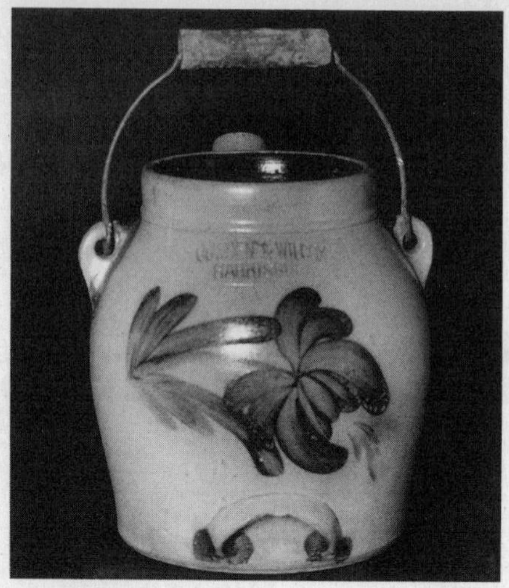

One gallon Cowden & Wilcox Harrisburg, PA
Generally ovoid in shape with metal bail handle and lug handle at base opposite pouring spout. Impressed with potter's imprint. Features large and boldly rendered floral design in cobalt blue. Very attractive. Minor chips. (COLLECTION OF BRAD MAXWELL)
Excellent Quality/Excellent Condition *$1,500–$2,000 (D)*

Bottles

One pint (Maker unknown)
Cylinder-shaped with slanted top. Decorated with large letter "A" in cobalt blue. Minor rim chip. (MARLIN G. DENLINGER AUCTION)
Very Good Quality/Excellent Condition *$105 (A)*

One pint (Maker unknown)
Cylinder-shaped with sloping shoulders. Blue-glazed at top. Base chip. (MARLIN G. DENLINGER AUCTION)
Good Quality/Excellent Condition *$45 (A)*

One pint (Maker unknown)
Cylinder-shaped with sloping shoulders. Brown-glazed at top. (MARLIN G. DENLINGER AUCTION)
Good Quality/Excellent Condition *$30 (A)*

One pint (Maker unknown)
Cylinder-shaped with sloping shoulders. Impressed with design that includes user's name—THE SPEYERS LION BREWERY, NEW YORK—and the figure of a lion. (HARMER ROOKE GALLERIES)
Very Good Quality/Excellent Condition *$100 (A)*

One quart (Maker unknown)
Cylinder-shaped with slanted shoulders. Banded in cobalt blue below neck. Stamped S. S. KNICKERBOCKER. (ARTHUR AUCTIONEERING)
Very Good Quality/Excellent Condition *$90 (A)*

One quart (Maker unknown)
Cylinder-shaped with slanted shoulders. Cobalt blue band with incised lines below neck. Stamped HYDE PARK. (ARTHUR AUCTIONEERING)
Very Good Quality/Very Good Condition *$150 (A)*

One quart (Maker unknown)
Cylinder-shaped with slanted shoulders. Top trimmed in cobalt blue. Stamped with initials J.H.W. Small rim chip. (ARTHUR AUCTIONEERING)
Very Good Quality/Very Good Condition *$40 (A)*

Bowls

One gallon S. Blair Cortland, NY
Rounded milk pan with lug handles. Impressed with potter's imprint. Small floral decoration in cobalt blue. Minor rim chips. (ARTHUR AUCTIONEERING)
Very Good Quality/Excellent Condition *$450 (A)*

One gallon Sipe & Sons Williamsport, PA
Rounded, wide-mouthed cream pot. Impressed with potter's imprint. Small cobalt blue floral decoration. Rim chip. (ARTHUR AUCTIONEERING)
Very Good Quality/Excellent Condition *$160 (A)*

One gallon (Maker unknown)
Slanted sides with pouring spout. Classified as a milk pan. Simple floral decoration at front and back in cobalt blue. Hairline crack at back. (ARTHUR AUCTIONEERING)
Good Quality/Excellent Condition *$300 (A)*

(Capacity unknown) Paul Cushman Albany, NY
Brown-glazed, slightly ovoid in shape, with lug handles. Classified as a milk bowl or milk crock. Potter's name impressed in block letters below rim. Dates to first decades of nineteenth century. (COLLECTION OF WILLARD E. GRANDE)
Excellent Quality/Excellent Condition *$3,000 (D)*

Two gallon Nathan Porter West Troy, NY
Low and wide-mouthed with lug handles and small pouring spout. Specifically, a milk bowl or milk pan, used in separating cream from milk. Impressed with potter's mark and numeral "2." Minor chips. (COLLECTION OF WILLARD E. GRANDE)
Excellent Quality/Excellent Condition *$450 (D)*

Churns

Two gallon J. P. Bodie SC
Cylinder-shaped with rounded shoulders and runny alkaline glaze. Impressed J. P. BODIE MAKER. Dates to about 1880. Rim chip; several handle chips. Rare. (HARMER ROOKE GALLERIES)
Superior Quality/Excellent Condition *$400 (A)*

Two gallon S. T. Brewer Havana, NY
Slightly ovoid in shape with lug handles. Impressed with maker's mark and numeral "2." Floral decoration in cobalt blue. Complete with dasher. (ARTHUR AUCTIONEERING)
Excellent Quality/Excellent Condition *$1,025 (A)*

Two gallon F. B. Norton Co. Worcester, MA
Slightly ovoid in shape with lug handles. Impressed with potter's imprint and numeral "2." Somewhat blurred decoration in cobalt blue features "Worcester parrot" seated on a leafy branch. Some kiln damage. (COLLECTION OF WILLARD E. GRANDE)
Very Good Quality/Very Good Condition *$1,800 (D)*

Three gallon A. Conrad New Geneva, PA
Slightly slanted sides with lug handle. Stenciled with potter's name and address, and with attractive free-hand floral decorations. (ARTHUR AUCTIONEERING)
Excellent Quality/Excellent Condition *$200 (A)*

Three gallon (Maker unknown)
Somewhat bulbous in shape with brownish green Albany-type glaze. One strap handle; one lug handle. Incised with a large numeral "3." Long vertical crack. Attributed to J. F. Hunt, Rusk County, TX. Dates to about 1880. From the collection of Georgeanna Greer. (HARMER ROOKE GALLERIES)
Excellent Quality/Excellent Condition *$85 (A)*

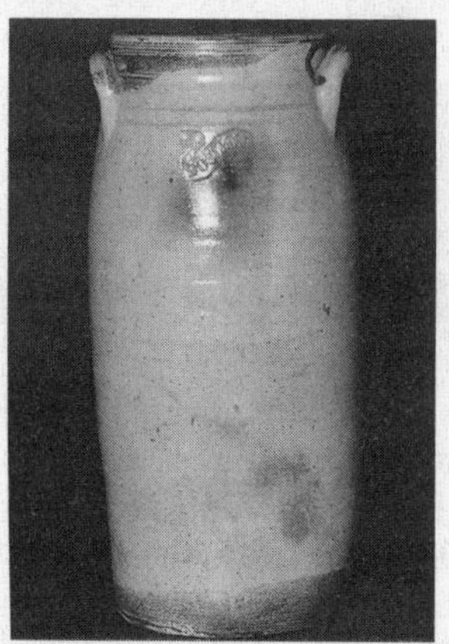

Three gallon (Maker unknown)
Tall, very slightly ovoid in form, with flared neck and lug handles. Decorated with the impressed word BOSTON enclosed in banner. Believed to be the work of Fred Carpenter, a Charlestown, MA, potter. (COLLECTION OF BRAD MAXWELL)
Excellent Quality/Excellent Condition *$2,500–$3,000 (D)*

Three gallon J. Burger & Co. Rochester, NY
Slightly ovoid in form with lug handles. Impressed with potter's imprint. Decorated in cobalt blue with large numeral "3" enclosed in a pair of ferns. Repaired crack. (ARTHUR AUCTIONEERING)
Excellent Quality/Good Condition *$125 (A)*

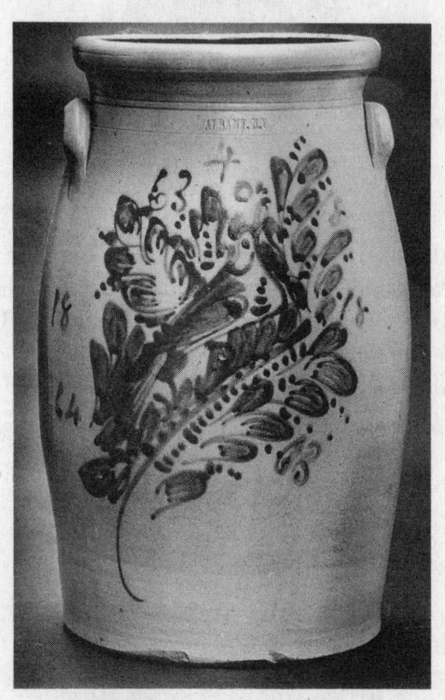

Four gallon Albany Stoneware Factory Albany, NY
Tall, slightly ovoid in shape with lug handles. ALBANY, N.Y. impressed near top. Involved design in cobalt blue depicts a long-billed bird amidst leaves, flowers, and branches, and numerals "18," "63," and "64" repeated a number of times. Some base chips. (COLLECTION OF BETTY AND JOEL SCHATZBERG)
Superior Quality/Excellent Condition *$10,000 (D)*

Four gallon N. Clark, Jr. Athens, NY
Slightly ovoid in form with lug handles. Impressed with potter's imprint. Large flower-and-leaf design rendered in cobalt blue. Cracked; metal band at base. (MARLIN G. DENLINGER AUCTION)
Excellent Quality/Good Condition *$100 (A)*

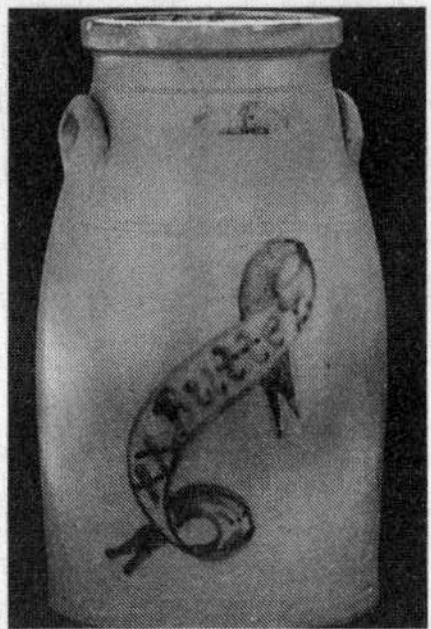

Four gallon Seymour & Bosworth Hartford, CT
Tall, cylinder-shaped, with tapered neck and lug handles. Impressed with potter's mark and numeral "4." Decorated with artful banner in cobalt blue within which the word "Butter" has been printed. (COLLECTION OF JACK AND PAT MCMACKIN)
Excellent Quality/Excellent Condition *$600–$800 (D)*

Four gallon E. & L. P. Norton Bennington, VT
Tall and slightly ovoid in shape with lug handles. Impressed with potter's imprint and large numeral "4." Bold and elaborate floral spray rendered in dark cobalt blue. (MARLIN G. DENLINGER AUCTION)
Excellent Quality/Fine Condition *$1,450 (A)*

Four gallon (Maker unknown)
Tall, tending toward a barrel shape. Lug handles dabbed with blue. Cobalt blue design depicts thick-trunked, straight-branched pine tree. Dates from 1810 to 1830. (COLLECTION OF JACK AND PAT MCMACKIN)
Excellent Quality/Excellent Condition *$1,200–$1,500 (D)*

Five gallon Hubbell & Chesebro Geddes, NY
Slightly ovoid in form with lug handles. With lid. Impressed with potter's imprint and large numeral "5." Outstanding cobalt blue decoration—handsome, long-maned prancing lion adorned with small poika dots. Small hairline crack. (ARTHUR AUCTIONEERING)
Superior Quality/Excellent Condition *$3,800 (A)*

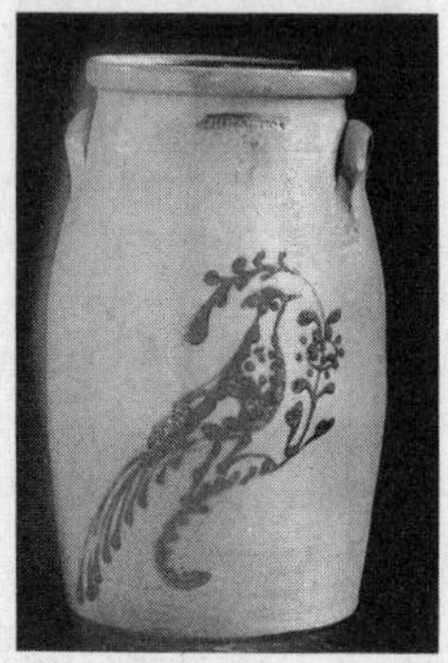

Five gallon Whites Utica, NY
Tends toward barrel shape, with boldly applied bird design below potter's imprint. Lug handles. Hairline cracks in front and at side. (COLLECTION OF WILLARD E. GRANDE)
Very Good Quality/Good Condition *$1,100 (D)*

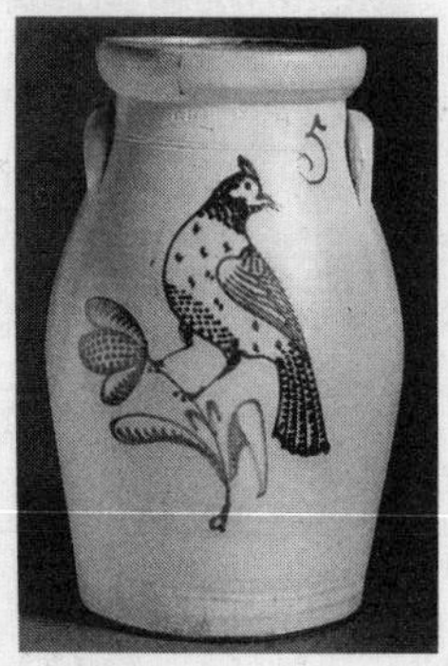

Five gallon T. Harrington
Ovoid in shape with lug handles. Impressed with potter's name. Design features boldly drawn partridge or other game bird perched on a delicate branch. The cobalt blue is thick and dark. (LITCHFIELD AUCTION GALLERY)
Excellent Quality/Excellent Condition *$4,000–$5,000 (D)*

Six gallon A. O. Whittemore Havana, NY
Slightly ovoid in shape with lug handles. Impressed with potter's name and numeral "6." Large, attractive floral design in cobalt blue. Tight crack at back; hairline cracks. (ARTHUR AUCTIONEERING)
Excellent Quality/Very Good Condition *$175 (A)*

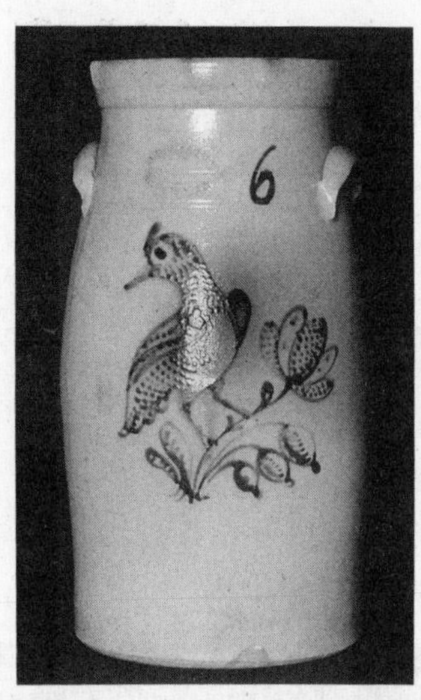

Six gallon J. Burger, Jr. Rochester, NY
Tall, slightly bulbous, with lug handles. Impressed with potter's imprint. Features sprightly game bird on leafy branch rendered in dark cobalt blue. Small rim chip. (COLLECTION OF BRAD MAXWELL)
Excellent Quality/Excellent Condition *$5,000–$6,000 (D)*

Crocks

Two quart (Maker unknown)
A low-sided cake crock with lug handles. Front decorated with cobalt blue squiggles beneath impressed numeral "2." Believed to be the work of Somerset Pottery of Somerset, MA. (COLLECTION OF DALE FARRELL)
Very Good Quality/Good Condition *$1,250–1,500 (D)*

One gallon (Maker unknown)
Ovoid in shape with lug handles. Floral design in wide-brushed cobalt blue strokes. (MARLIN G. DENLINGER AUCTION)
Excellent Quality/Fine Condition *$150 (A)*

One gallon (Maker unknown)
Ovoid in shape with brown glaze. Unusual blue and ocher leaf-and-berries decoration. Possibly the work of Edmands & Co., Boston potters from 1812 to 1905. Minor rim chips. (COLLECTION OF EARL CURRY)
Excellent Quality/Excellent Condition *$800 (D)*

One gallon (Maker unknown)
Butter crock with lid. Straight-sided with lug handles. Attractive floral decoration in cobalt blue at both front and back. (ARTHUR AUCTIONEERING)
Excellent Quality/Excellent Condition *$550 (A)*

One gallon H. M. Whitman Havana, NY
Straight-sided with lug handles and single band near top. Impressed with maker's mark. Unusual design features pair of crossed fish in cobalt blue. (COLLECTION OF BETTY AND JOEL SCHATZBERG)
Superior Quality/Fine Condition *$15,000–$18,000 (D)*

One gallon (Maker unknown)
Ovoid in form. No handles. Attributed to Nichols & Co., Williamsport, PA. Decorated with simple free-hand drawing of a flower. Minor rim chips. (ARTHUR AUCTIONEERING)
Very Good Quality/Excellent Condition *$90 (A)*

One gallon White's Utica, NY
Ovoid in form with lug handles. Impressed with potter's name. Features somewhat cartoony design of small dark-winged bird rendered in cobalt blue. Hole drilled in bottom. (MARLIN G. DENLINGER AUCTION)
Excellent Quality/Excellent Condition *$175 (A)*

One gallon (Maker unknown)
Ovoid in form with lug handles. Decoration in cobalt blue had a Civil War theme—crossed flags and word "Union" in script. Highly desirable. (COLLECTION OF BETTY AND JOEL SCHATZBERG)
Superior Quality/Excellent Condition *$15,000 (D)*

One gallon (Maker unknown)
Straight-sided butter crock with lug handles. Complete with lid. Decorated front and back in cobalt blue. Hairline crack in lid. Repaired crack in crock. (ARTHUR AUCTIONEERING)
Excellent Quality/Good Condition *$300 (A)*

One gallon J. & E. Norton Bennington, VT
Ovoid in shape with lug handles. Impressed with potter's imprint. Small design of bird perched on log in cobalt blue. Minor chip. (MARLIN G. DENLINGER AUCTION)
Excellent Quality/Excellent Condition *$500 (A)*

One gallon (Maker unknown)
Ovoid in shape with free-standing handles and double band near top. Described as a cream pot. Handle bases are dabbed with cobalt blue. BOSTON impressed at front. Believed to be the work of Jonathan Fenton, eighteenth-century Boston potter. Attractively decorated with incised picture of codfish finished in cobalt blue. One handle has hairline crack. Outstanding. (COLLECTION OF BRAD MAXWELL)
Superior Quality/Excellent Condition *$4,500 (D)*

One gallon (Maker unknown)
Slightly ovoid sausage crock. Possibly from Williamsport, PA, potter. Cobalt blue floral decoration at front. Minor chip; some flaking. (ARTHUR AUCTIONEERING)
Good Quality/Good Condition *$100 (A)*

One gallon (Maker unknown)
Ovoid in shape with two-tone brown glaze (from being twice dipped). Double band between neck and body. BOSTON impressed in printed letters below neck. Small firing imperfections. Slight base chipping. (COLLECTION OF EARL CURRY)
Excellent Quality/Good Condition *$300 (D)*

One gallon D. Roberts & Co. Utica, NY
Ovoid in form with lug handles. Impressed with potter's name. Floral design in cobalt blue. Minor base chips. Some discoloration. (MARLIN G. DENLINGER AUCTION)
Excellent Quality/Excellent Condition *$250 (A)*

One gallon (Maker unknown)
Straight-sided butter crock with lid. Simply decorated in cobalt blue at front and back. Chips on lid and handle. Large areas of discoloration. (ARTHUR AUCTIONEERING)
Good Quality/Poor Condition *$130 (A)*

One gallon Evan R. Jones Pittston, PA
Straight-sided cake crock with lug handles. Impressed with potter's imprint. Large, leafy tulip rendered horizontally in cobalt blue. (MARLIN G. DENLINGER AUCTION)
Excellent Quality/Excellent Condition *$275 (A)*

One and one-half gallon E. & B. Norton Co. Worcester, MA
A low-sided cake crock, impressed with maker's mark and capacity designation—"1½." Elaborate drawing of turreted building, believed to be the Oread Collegiate Institute, a women's college once located on Castle Hill in Worcester. Hairline crack near bottom. Exceptional. (COLLECTION OF BETTY AND JOEL SCHATZBERG)
Superior Quality/Excellent Condition *$15,000–$20,000 (D)*

One and one-half gallon M. T. Williams New Geneva, PA
Ovoid in form. No handles. Stenciled with potter's name and floral decoration. Large free-hand rendering of "1½." Minor base chips. (ARTHUR AUCTIONEERING)
Excellent Quality/Excellent Condition *$125 (A)*

Two gallon Redwing Union Stoneware Co. Redwing, MN
Straight-sided. No handles. Impressed with potter's name near base. Hand-drawn numeral "2" near top. (ARTHUR AUCTIONEERING)
Good Quality/Excellent Condition *$30 (A)*

Two gallon E. Norton & Co. Bennington, VT
Straight-sided cake crock with lug handles. Tan in color. Impressed with potter's imprint and numeral "2." Floral decoration in cobalt blue. Minor chips. (ARTHUR AUCTIONEERING)
Excellent Quality/Excellent Condition *$200 (A)*

Two gallon Athens Pottery Athens, NY
Slightly sloping sides with lug handles. ATHENS POTTERY impressed near top. Features floral decoration in cobalt blue with the year "1893" incorporated in the design. (A pottery is known to have operated in Athens, New York, from 1893 to 1900.) Rim chips. (COLLECTION OF WILLARD E. GRANDE)
Very Good Quality/Excellent Condition *$550 (D)*

Two gallon Cowden & Wilcox Harrisburg, PA
Low-sided cake crock with lug handles. Impressed with potter's imprint. Banded near top. Bold floral decoration in cobalt blue. (ARTHUR AUCTIONEERING)
Excellent Quality/Excellent Condition *$400 (A)*

Two gallon C. Hart & Son Sherburne, NY
Straight-sided with lug handles. Impressed with potter's name and numeral "2." "Emma" blazoned in cobalt blue script across front. (MARLIN G. DENLINGER AUCTION)
Excellent Quality/Excellent Condition *$170 (A)*

Two gallon White's Utica, NY
Squat ovoid in form with lug handles. Impressed with potter's name and large numeral "2." Features folksy cobalt blue drawing of a man in a fedora examining a small tree or large flower. Repaired rim chip. Interesting. (COLLECTION OF WILLARD E. GRANDE)
Excellent Quality/Excellent Condition *$4,200 (D)*

Two gallon F. Stetzenmeyer Rochester, NY
Slightly ovoid in form with lug handles. Impressed with potter's imprint. Multileaf design and numeral "2" rendered in cobalt blue. Hairline crack; minor chip. (MARLIN G. DENLINGER AUCTION)
Excellent Quality/Excellent Condition *$250 (A)*

Two gallon (Maker unknown)
Straight-sided; no handles. Bears large folksy drawing in cobalt blue of a long-nosed man running, a bag on a stick over one shoulder. In blue script are the words "for Pike's Peak." Probably of Ohio origin. Some kiln discoloration. Odd. (COLLECTION OF WILLARD E. GRANDE)
Excellent Quality/Excellent Condition *$4,500 (D)*

Two gallon O. H. Seymour Hartford, CT
Slightly slanted sides with lug handles. Impressed with potter's imprint and numeral "2." "Liberty and Equality" blazoned across front in cobalt blue. Hairline crack. (MARLIN G. DENLINGER AUCTION)
Superior Quality/Excellent Condition *$1,000 (A)*

Two gallon J. & E. Norton Bennington, VT
Straight-sided with lug handles. Impressed with potter's imprint and numeral "2." Very large, bold, and vivid cobalt blue design features reclining stag between two rail fences and a pair of trees. (MARLIN G. DENLINGER AUCTION)
Superior Quality/Excellent Condition *$3,300 (A)*

Two gallon J. M. Crafts & Co. Whately, MA
Straight-sided with lug handles. Double-banded near top. Impressed with potter's imprint and numeral "2." Decorated in cobalt blue with small drawing of leaping rabbit. Somewhat unusual. (COLLECTION OF WILLARD E. GRANDE)
Excellent Quality/Excellent Condition *$1,500 (D)*

Two gallon C. Hart Sherburne, NY
Gently sloping sides with lug handles. Impressed with potter's imprint and large numeral "2." Attractive floral design in cobalt blue. (MARLIN G. DENLINGER AUCTION)
Excellent Quality/Excellent Condition *$190 (A)*

Two gallon J. Burger Rochester, NY
Straight-sided with lug handles. Impressed with potter's name. Large hand-embossed numeral "2" appears to the right of the imprint. Design in cobalt blue features a sunflower with a grinning face. Some hairline cracks and flaking. (COLLECTION OF WILLARD E. GRANDE)
Excellent Quality/Good Condition *$2,500 (D)*

Two gallon (Maker unknown)
Straight-sided with lug handles. Impressed with numeral "2." Potter not known. Elaborate cobalt blue rendering of glass vase filled with flowers. Hairline crack. (MARLIN G. DENLINGER AUCTION)
Excellent Quality/Excellent Condition *$150 (A)*

Two gallon West Troy Pottery West Troy, NY
Impressed with potter's mark and numeral "2." Sustained deep dents at the front and one side during firing. Bird decoration in cobalt blue is blurred. (COLLECTION OF WILLARD E. GRANDE)
Good Quality/Poor Condition *$750 (D)*

Two gallon (Maker unknown)
Straight-sided with lug handles. Potter not known. Numeral "2" and year "1867" rendered in cobalt blue. Minor base chips. (MARLIN G. DENLINGER AUCTION)
Very Good Quality/Excellent Condition *$110 (A)*

Two gallon J. Mantell Penn Yan, NY
Slightly sloping sides with lug handles. Impressed with potter's name and large "2." Double band near top. Large floral design in cobalt blue. (COLLECTION OF BRAD MAXWELL)
Excellent Quality/Excellent Condition *$500–$650 (D)*

Two gallon J. & E. Norton Co. Bennington, VT
Ovoid in form with lug handles. Impressed with potter's imprint and large numeral "2." Handsome double-flower design rendered in cobalt blue. (MARLIN G. DENLINGER AUCTION)
Excellent Quality/Excellent Condition *$220 (A)*

Two gallon C. Boynton & Co. Troy, NY
Ovoid in form with lug handles. Impressed with potter's mark. Wide-brushed leaf design in cobalt blue. Crack at back. (MARLIN G. DENLINGER AUCTION)
Excellent Quality/Very Good Condition *$100 (A)*

Two gallon O. M. Seymour Hartford, CT
Straight-sided with lug handles. Impressed with maker's mark and large numeral "2." Bears squiggly design in cobalt blue, said to resemble a caduceus, symbol of the medical profession. (COLLECTION OF MARY MAZENS)
Excellent Quality/Excellent Condition *$275 (A)*

Two and one-half gallon Paul Cushman Albany, NY
Classic ovoid in form with double band near top. Incised on both sides with PAUL CUSHMAN STONEWARE FACTORY in large type. One of the lug handles is missing. Small base chips. (COLLECTION OF WILLARD E. GRANDE)
Excellent Quality/Good Condition *$1,800 (D)*

Three gallon (Maker unknown)
Straight-sided with lug handles. Somewhat folksy design in cobalt blue features bushy-tailed bird on large stump. (MARLIN G. DENLINGER AUCTION)
Excellent Quality/Excellent Condition *$325 (A)*

Three gallon West Troy Pottery West Troy, NY
Straight-sided with lug handles and double band near top. Impressed with maker's mark. Striking incised design depicts pair of sprightly circus horses against an imaginative background rendered in cobalt blue. Dates from 1879 to 1880. (COLLECTION OF WILLARD E. GRANDE)
Superior Quality/Excellent Condition *$18,000 (D)*

Three gallon J. & E. Norton Co. Bennington, VT
Straight-sided with lug handles. Impressed with potter's imprint. Bold double-flower decoration rendered in cobalt blue. (MARLIN G. DENLINGER AUCTION)
Excellent Quality/Excellent Condition *$150 (A)*

Three gallon T. Harrington Lyons, NY
Straight-sided with lug handles. Impressed with potter's imprint. Eye-catching design in cobalt blue that covers the front, top to bottom, depicts unusual eight-pointed star with half-moon center and numeral "3" at each side. Fairly rare. (COLLECTION OF WILLARD E. GRANDE)
Excellent Quality/Excellent Condition *$6,500 (D)*

Three gallon J. F. Brayton Utica, NY
Ovoid in form, with lug handles and triple band near top. Impressed with potter's imprint. Large numeral "3" and bright floral design comprise decoration. Minor rim chips. (COLLECTION OF BILL SULLIVAN)
Good Quality/Excellent Condition *$250 (D)*

Three gallon C. Hart & Son Sherburne, NY
Straight-sided with lug handles. Impressed with potter's imprint. Bold floral decoration in cobalt blue. Large areas of discoloration. Hairline cracks at back. (ARTHUR AUCTIONEERING)
Good Quality/Poor Condition *$100 (A)*

Three gallon J. & E. Norton Bennington, VT
Straight-sided with lug handles. Impressed with potter's imprint and numeral "3." Decoration features a stag, standing and alert, depicted amidst low shrubs. Slumping at one side. (COLLECTION OF WILLARD E. GRANDE)
Excellent Quality/Good Condition *$5,000 (D)*

Three gallon Cowden & Wilcox Harrisburg, PA
Ovoid in form with lug handles. Impressed with potter's imprint and numeral "3." Bold floral design in cobalt blue. (MARLIN G. DENLINGER AUCTION)
Excellent Quality/Fine Condition *$575 (A)*

Three gallon Burger & Co. Rochester, NY
Gently sloping sides with lug handles. Impressed with potter's imprint. Bold double-flower design rendered in cobalt blue. Minor repair to one handle. (MARLIN G. DENLINGER AUCTION)
Excellent Quality/Excellent Condition *$350 (A)*

Three gallon New York Stoneware Co. Fort Edward, NY
Straight-sided with lug handles. Impressed with maker's mark and large numeral "3," but imprint appears near base, not top. Features cobalt blue depiction of long-tailed bird perched on a four-leaved branch. Some rim chips, kiln discoloration. Different. (COLLECTION OF WILLARD E. GRANDE)
Excellent Quality/Excellent Condition *$1,100 (D)*

Three gallon T. F. Connolly New Brunswick, NY
Straight-sided with lug handles. Impressed with maker's imprint. Large and handsome bird in cobalt blue. (ARTHUR AUCTIONEERING)
Excellent Quality/Excellent Condition *$675 (A)*

Three gallon Seymour & Bosworth Hartford, CT
Slightly sloping sides with lug handles. Impressed with potter's imprint and large numeral "3." Features simple pastoral scene in cobalt blue. (COLLECTION OF BETTY AND JOEL SCHATZBERG)
Excellent Quality/Excellent Condition *$5,000–$7,000 (D)*

Three gallon William Roberts Binghamton, NY
Slightly sloping sides with lug handles. Impressed with potter's imprint and numeral "3." Folksy drawing in cobalt blue of bearded, curly headed man wearing a top hat. Hairline crack; some rim chips and kiln discoloration. (COLLECTION OF WILLARD E. GRANDE)
Excellent Quality/Good Condition *$3,300 (D)*

Three gallon J. Burger, Jr. Rochester, NY
Gently sloping sides with lug handles. Impressed with potter's imprint. Rendering in cobalt blue of intertwined leaves and numeral "3." (MARLIN G. DENLINGER AUCTION)
Excellent Quality/Excellent Condition *$300 (A)*

Three gallon E. & L. P. Norton & Co. Bennington, VT
Slightly slanted sides with lug handles. Intricate triple-leaf design rendered in cobalt blue. Crack at back. (MARLIN G. DENLINGER AUCTION)
Excellent Quality/Very Good Condition *$100 (A)*

Three gallon J. & E. Norton Bennington, VT
Straight-sided with lug handles. Impressed with potter's imprint and numeral "3." Entire area between handles in front is filled with a barnyard scene in cobalt blue—a rooster perched on a fence turns to look at a small cluster of farm buildings. Very rare. (COLLECTION OF WILLARD GRANDE)
Superior Quality/Excellent Condition *$12,500 (D)*

Three gallon (Maker unknown)
Straight-sided with lug handles. Features folksy drawing in cobalt blue of man from waist up that owner says is "an Indian, a Mohawk, wearing buckskins." Attributed to C. W. Braun, a pre–Civil War, Buffalo, New York, potter. (COLLECTION OF BETTY AND JOEL SCHATZBERG)
Superior Quality/Excellent Condition *$8,000–$12,000 (D)*

Three gallon E. & L. P. Norton Bennington, VT
Straight-sided with lug handles. Impressed with potter's imprint. Large and handsome bird perched on leafy branch rendered in cobalt blue. Minor flaking; some discoloration. (MARLIN G. DENLINGER AUCTION)
Excellent Quality/Very Good Condition *$200 (A)*

Three gallon William A. Macquoid NY City
Straight-sided with lug handles. Single band near top. Impressed with the numeral "3" and the potter's name and address, W. A. MACQUOID & CO., POTTERYWORKS [*sic*]. LITTLE WEST 12TH ST., NY. Features cobalt blue design of a sailing ship and a printed phrase proclaiming "Don't give up the ship," and "Capt. Law." (Captain Lawrence). (COLLECTION OF WILLARD E. GRANDE)
Superior Quality/Very Good Condition *$22,000 (D)*

Three gallon Haxstun & Co. Fort Edward, NY
Straight-sided with lug handles. Impressed with potter's imprint and numeral "3." Bold design in cobalt blue of plumpish bird perched on tree branch. (MARLIN G. DENLINGER AUCTION)
Excellent Quality/Excellent Condition *$325 (A)*

Three gallon T. Harrington Lyons, NY
Slightly ovoid in shape with lug handles. Impressed with potter's imprint. The piece has been named "Starface." In dark cobalt blue, it depicts an eight-pointed star that covers the front from top to bottom. In the center of the star, a human face has been drawn. Numeral "3" appears on each side of design. Striking. (COLLECTION OF WILLARD E. GRANDE)
Superior Quality/Excellent Condition *$6,000 (D)*

Three gallon (Maker unknown)
Straight-sided with lug handles. Design in cobalt blue features plump chicken pecking at feed. (MARLIN G. DENLINGER AUCTION)
Excellent Quality/Fine Condition *$550 (A)*

Three gallon M. Woodruff Cortland, NY
Slightly sloping sides with lug handles. Impressed with potter's imprint and numeral "3"; also with x trademark used by Woodruff to identify his ware. Large floral design in cobalt blue. Some kiln discoloration. (COLLECTION OF BILL SULLIVAN)
Very Good Quality/Excellent Condition *$275 (D)*

Three gallon West Troy Pottery West Troy, NY
Straight-sided with lug handles. No maker's mark but attributed to West Troy, New York, pottery. Elaborate cobalt blue design features a short-tailed elephant with upraised trunk striding from left to right. Very rare. (COLLECTION OF WILLARD E. GRANDE)
Superior Quality/Fine Condition *$15,000 (D)*

Three gallon West Troy Pottery West Troy, NY
Straight-sided with lug handles. Impressed with potter's mark and numeral "3." Features design of fast-striding elephant with upraised trunk moving from right to left, depicted in reverse—in white against a background of cobalt blue vegetation. Very rare. (COLLECTION OF WILLARD E. GRANDE)
Superior Quality/Fine Condition *$15,000 (D)*

Three gallon Fort Edward Stoneware Co. Fort Edward, NY
Straight-sided with lug handles. Impressed with potter's imprint. Bold design in cobalt blue features long-tailed bird perched on a floral branch. Crack at back. (MARLIN G. DENLINGER AUCTION)
Excellent Quality/Very Good Condition *$120 (A)*

Three gallon (Maker unknown)
Straight-sided with lug handles. Design in cobalt blue features large poppylike flower. Base chip. (MARLIN G. DENLINGER AUCTION)
Excellent Quality/Excellent Condition *$175 (A)*

Four gallon New York Stoneware Co. Fort Edward, NY
Straight-sided with lug handles. Impressed with potter's name and numeral "4." Very folksy cobalt blue line drawing depicting two men, barely more than stick figures, in animated conversation. One man is identified as "Pat Byrace." Rim chips. (COLLECTION OF WILLARD E. GRANDE)
Superior Quality/Excellent Condition *$6,500 (D)*

Four gallon Ballard Brothers Burlington, VT
Straight-sided with potter's imprint and numeral "4." Exciting floral design in cobalt blue covers entire front from handle to handle, even partially obliterating maker's mark. Unusual. Handle chip and serious crack at back. (COLLECTION OF WILLARD E. GRANDE)
Excellent Quality/Good Condition *$1,800 (D)*

Four gallon White's Utica, NY
Straight-sided with lug handles. Impressed with potter's imprint and numeral "4." Cobalt blue rendering of speckled, long-tailed bird on slim branch. Some discoloration. (MARLIN G. DENLINGER AUCTION)
Excellent Quality/Excellent Condition *$375 (A)*

Four gallon O. H. Seymour Hartford, CT
Impressed with potter's mark and numeral "4." Features the maxim "Nothing venture [*sic*], nothing have," in cobalt blue script, with swirls beneath. Unusual. (COLLECTION OF JACK AND PAT MCMACKIN)
Excellent Quality/Excellent Condition *$1,500–$2,000 (D)*

Four gallon West Troy Pottery West Troy, NY
Straight-sided with lug handles. Impressed with potter's imprint and numeral "4." Cobalt blue rendering of plump chicken pecking at feed. Some discoloration. (MARLIN G. DENLINGER AUCTION)
Excellent Quality/Excellent Condition *$375 (A)*

Four gallon Somerset Potter's Works Somerset, NJ
Straight-sided with lug handles. Impressed with potter's imprint and numeral "4." Design rendered in reverse—a long-tailed pony in white depicted against a dark cobalt blue background. Extensive repairs to rim and one handle. (COLLECTION OF WILLARD E. GRANDE)
Excellent Quality/Good Condition *$6,500 (D)*

Four gallon T. H. Brington Lyons, NY
Straight-sided with lug handles, and single and double bands near top. Impressed with potter's name. Striking cobalt blue design features a large lion, its head turned, looking to the rear, as it prances forward. Design also includes large numeral "4" in cobalt blue. Very rare. (COLLECTION OF BETTY AND JOEL SCHATZBERG)
Superior Quality/Excellent Condition *$30,000–$45,000 (D)*

Four gallon White's Utica, NY
Straight-sided. Impressed with potter's imprint. Cobalt blue decoration featuring large bird and "1878." Handles missing; cracked; flaked. (ARTHUR AUCTIONEERING)
Very Good Quality/Poor Condition *$180 (A)*

Four gallon Haxstun & Co. Fort Edward, NY
Straight-sided with lug handles. Impressed with potter's name and large numeral "4." Unusual design in cobalt blue features a rustic house and surrounding yard with small trees and shrubs. (COLLECTION OF WILLARD E. GRANDE)
Superior Quality/Excellent Condition *$6,000 (D)*

Four gallon Burger & Lang Rochester, NY
Straight-sided with lug handles. Impressed with potter's imprint. Numeral "4" and simple but attractive flower-and-leaf design rendered in cobalt blue. Minor rim chips. (MARLIN G. DENLINGER AUCTION)
Excellent Quality/Excellent Condition *$170 (A)*

Four gallon W. A. Lewis Galesville, NY
Straight-sided with lug handles. Impressed with potter's imprint and numeral "4." Bears very folksy cobalt blue drawing of the clustered factory buildings where Lewis's pottery was produced from 1857 to 1860. Extremely rare. Small crack at back. (COLLECTION OF WILLARD E. GRANDE)
Superior Quality/Excellent Condition *$40,000 (D)*

Four gallon J. Norton & Co. Bennington, VT
Straight-sided with lug handles and triple band near top. Impressed with maker's name and large numeral "4." Bold cobalt blue design depicts pair of plump birds on tree branch. Minor rim chips. (COLLECTION OF BRAD MAXWELL)
Excellent Quality/Excellent Condition *$1,800–$2,000 (D)*

Four gallon White's Utica, NY
Straight-sided with lug handles. Impressed with potter's imprint. Long-tailed, long-billed bird rendered in cobalt blue. Crack at back. (MARLIN G. DENLINGER AUCTION)
Excellent Quality/Good Condition *$150 (A)*

Four gallon J. Norton & Co. Bennington, VT
Slightly ovoid in shape with lug handles. Double band a few inches below rim. Impressed with potter's imprint and numeral "4." Decorated in cobalt blue with double bird design. Hairline cracks in front. (COLLECTION OF WILLARD E. GRANDE)
Very Good Quality/Excellent Condition *$2,000 (D)*

Four gallon W. Roberts Binghamton, NY
Ovoid in form with lug handles. Impressed with potter's imprint and large numeral "4." Cobalt blue rendering of very large bird perched on a floral branch. Repaired flaking at back. (ARTHUR AUCTIONEERING)
Excellent Quality/Good Condition *$350 (A)*

Four gallon E. & L. P. Norton Bennington, VT
Straight-sided with lug handles. Impressed with potter's name. Attractive floral design in cobalt blue. Some kiln damage. (COLLECTION OF WILLARD E. GRANDE)
Very Good Quality/Very Good Condition *$500 (D)*

Four gallon (Maker unknown)
Ovoid in shape with lug handles. Attractive flower-and-leaf design rendered in cobalt blue. Also, blue band near top. Minor chips. (MARLIN G. DENLINGER AUCTION)
Excellent Quality/Excellent Condition *$400 (A)*

Four gallon O. L. & A. K. Ballard Burlington, VT
Straight-sided with lug handles. Impressed with potter's imprint. Very large and very bold design of long-tailed bird perched on tree branch. Hairline crack. (MARLIN G. DENLINGER AUCTION)
Excellent Quality/Excellent Condition *$425 (A)*

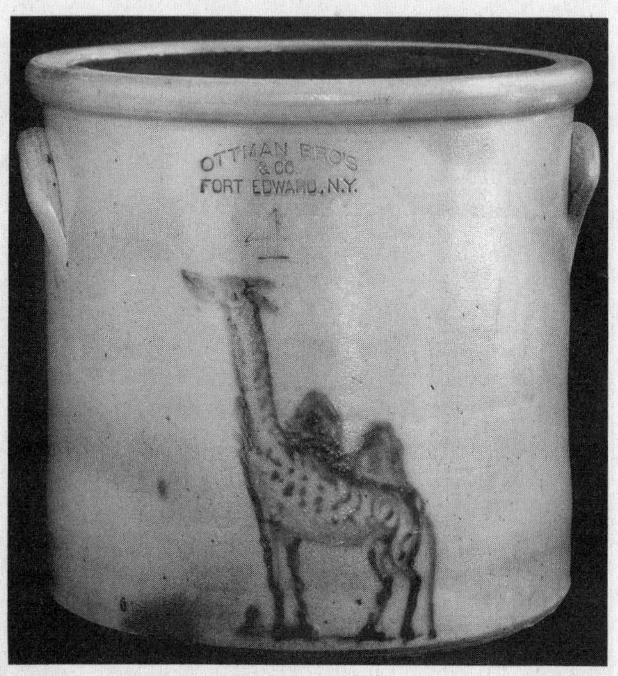

Four gallon Ottman Brothers & Co. Fort Edward, NY
Straight-sided with lug handles. Impressed with maker's imprint and large numeral "4." Highly prized because of the unique decoration—a cobalt blue drawing of a bizarre animal, either a camel with a very long neck or a giraffe with two humps. (COLLECTION OF WILLARD E. GRANDE)
Superior Quality/Excellent Condition *$10,000 (D)*

Four gallon (Maker unknown)
Straight-sided with lug handles. Attractive design in cobalt blue features young bird perched on tree branch. Some firing damage at back. (MARLIN G. DENLINGER AUCTION)
Excellent Quality/Excellent Condition *$150 (A)*

Four gallon J. McBurney Jordan, NY
Ovoid in shape with lug handles. Impressed with maker's mark. Features cobalt blue drawing of unusual bird. Quite appealing. Cracks at back. (COLLECTION OF WILLARD E. GRANDE)
Excellent Quality/Good Condition *$2,800 (D)*

Four gallon A. O. Whittemore Havana, NY
Slightly sloping sides with lug handles. Impressed with potter's mark: A. O. WHITTEMORE, HAVANA (now Montour Falls), N.Y. Unusual design in heavy, dark cobalt blue features a small house behind a lake or pond. Sizable grease stains. (COLLECTION OF BRAD MAXWELL)
Excellent Quality/Good Condition *$1,800–$2,000 (D)*

Four gallon White's Utica, NY
Straight-sided with lug handles. Impressed with potter's imprint and large numeral "4." Design in cobalt blue features plump, long-tailed bird perched on leafy branch. Hairline crack. (MARLIN G. DENLINGER AUCTION)
Excellent Quality/Excellent Condition *$250 (A)*

Four gallon Norton & Fenton Bennington, VT
Ovoid in shape with lug handles and single band near top. Impressed with maker's mark that is arranged in circular design surrounding large numeral "4." Triple-leaf decoration in cobalt blue. Dates from 1843 to 1845. (COLLECTION OF WILLARD E. GRANDE)
Excellent Quality/Excellent Condition *$850 (D)*

Four gallon New York Stoneware Co. Fort Edward, NY
Straight-sided with lug handles. Impressed with maker's name and numeral "4." Cobalt blue design depicts very plump bird perched on a leafy branch. Hairline crack and few rim chips. (COLLECTION OF WILLARD E. GRANDE)
Excellent Quality/Excellent Condition *$850 (D)*

Four gallon W. A. Lewis Galesville, NY
Straight-sided with lug handles. Impressed with potter's name and numeral "4." Superior design in cobalt blue features standing stag pictured between large and small trees. Crack at back. (MARLIN G. DENLINGER AUCTION)
Excellent Quality/Very Good Condition *$2,800 (A)*

Four gallon Somerset Pottery Works Somerset, MA
Straight-sided with lug handles and potter's imprint below the numeral "4." Features design of Jumbo, Barnum's famed elephant, and behind, her smaller offspring, both rendered in reverse, white on blue. The name "Jumbo" appears in block letters below the design. (COLLECTION OF WILLARD E. GRANDE)
Superior Quality/Good Condition *$6,500 (D)*

Four gallon S. Hart Fulton, NY
Slightly sloping sides with lug handles. Impressed with maker's mark. Design in cobalt blue features a cleverly drawn dog holding a basket in its mouth. Unusual. Crack in the back. (COLLECTION OF WILLARD E. GRANDE)
Excellent Quality/Good Condition *$3,600 (D)*

Four gallon C. W. Braun Buffalo, NY
Straight-sided with lug handles. Impressed with maker's name and large numeral "4." Heavily dotted cobalt blue design features a large turkey. Minor slumping near one handle. Hairline cracks. (COLLECTION OF WILLARD E. GRANDE)
Excellent Quality/Good Condition *$3,000 (D)*

Four gallon J. A. & C. W. Underwood Fort Edward, NY
Slightly ovoid in shape with lug handles. Impressed with potter's imprint and numeral "4." Exceptional design in dark cobalt blue features a large basket of flowers. Minor chips; two hairline cracks. (COLLECTION OF BETTY AND JOEL SCHATZBERG)
Superior Quality/Excellent Condition *$3,000–$4,000 (D)*

Five gallon T. Harrington Lyons, NY
Straight-sided with lug handles and double band near top. Impressed with maker's mark and large numeral "5." Decorated in deep cobalt blue with elaborate squiggles. (COLLECTION OF BILL SULLIVAN)
Excellent Quality/Excellent Condition *$275 (A)*

Five gallon Haxstun, Ottman & Co. Fort Edward, NY
Straight-sided with pair of lug handles. Design features a prancing stag against a background that includes a tall tree and a rustic fence. Stamped with potter's name and large numeral "5." (COLLECTION OF WILLARD E. GRANDE)
Superior Quality/Excellent Condition *$8,500 (D)*

Five gallon William E. Warner West Troy, NY
Straight-sided with lug handles. Impressed with potter's imprint and numeral "5." Large and striking symmetrical floral design in cobalt blue. Some rim and base chips. (COLLECTION OF WILLARD E. GRANDE)
Excellent Quality/Excellent Condition *$2,000 (D)*

Five gallon Haxstun Ottman & Co. Fort Edward, NY
Straight-sided with lug handles. Impressed with potter's imprint and numeral "5." Elaborate design in cobalt blue features leafy floral spray. Minor flaking. (MARLIN G. DENLINGER AUCTION)
Excellent Quality/Excellent Condition *$100 (A)*

Five gallon (Maker unknown)
Straight-sided with lug handles and a single band not far from rim. Handsome cobalt blue design that features a plump bird perched on a branch beneath a bower created of bird-foot tracks. Crack at back has been repaired. Unusual. (COLLECTION OF WILLARD E. GRANDE)
Excellent Quality/Good Condition *$1,500 (D)*

Five gallon Hubbell & Chesebro Geddes, NY
Straight-sided with lug handles. Impressed with potter's imprint. Bold flower and wreath design in cobalt blue. Repaired crack and minor chips. (ARTHUR AUCTIONEERING)
Excellent Quality/Good Condition *$160 (A)*

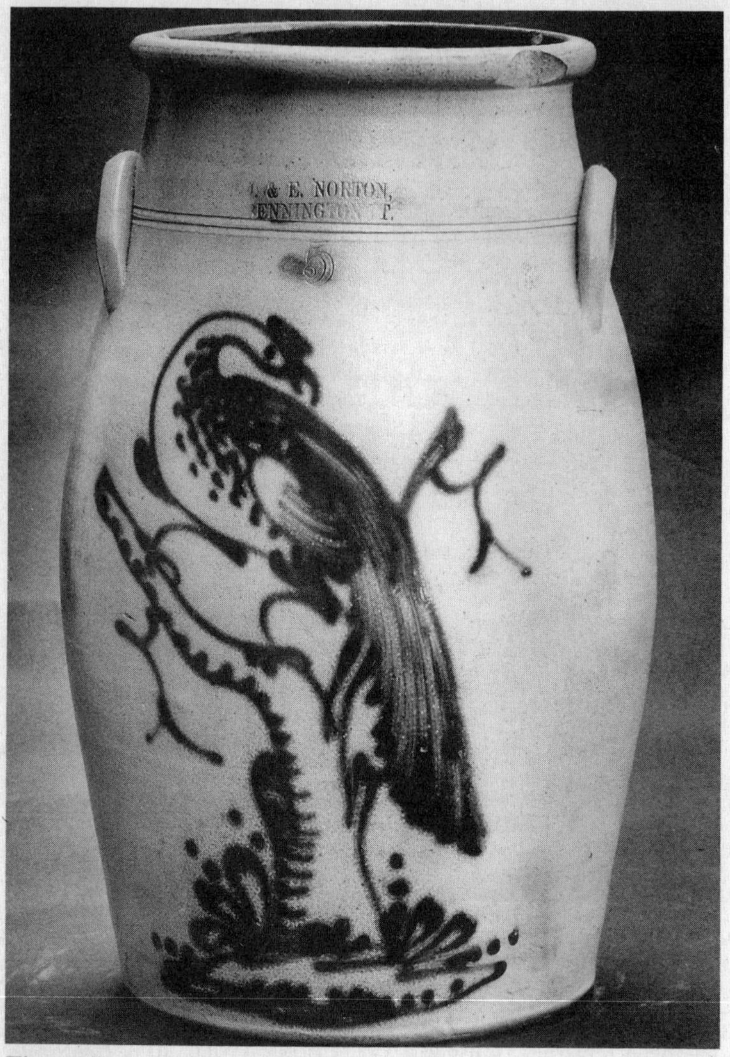

Five gallon J. & E. Norton Bennington, VT
Tends toward barrel shape with lug handles and double band near top. Impressed with potter's name and numeral "5." Bold, deep blue design covers front from top to bottom and depicts large and gaudy peacock perched on a double-limbed tree stump. Outstanding. (COLLECTION OF BETTY AND JOEL SCHATZBERG)
Superior Quality/Excellent Condition *$25,000 (D)*

Five gallon White's Utica, NY
Straight-sided crock with lug handles and double band near top. WHITE'S UTICA, in reverse, impressed at front. Imprint is incorporated in exceptional floral design in cobalt blue, which is crowned with leafy branches. Exceptional decoration. (COLLECTION OF JACK AND PAT MCMACKIN)
Superior Quality/Fine Condition *$2,500–$3,000 (D)*

Five gallon Haxstun & Co. Fort Edward, NY
Slightly slanted sides with lug handles. Impressed with potter's imprint and numeral "5." Floral design rendered in light cobalt blue. Hairline crack. (MARLIN G. DENLINGER AUCTION)
Excellent Quality/Excellent Condition *$120 (A)*

Six gallon William Macquoid NY City
Straight-sided with lug handles and single band near top. Impressed with maker's name and street address—LITTLE WEST 12TH ST.—and large numeral "6." Striking cobalt blue design featuring eagle with widely spread wings atop a decorated shield. Minor rim chips. Exceptional. (COLLECTION OF WILLARD E. GRANDE)
Superior Quality/Excellent Condition *$9,500 (D)*

Six gallon Ottman Bros. & Co. Fort Edward, NY
Straight-sided with lug handles. Impressed with potter's name and numeral "6." Design in cobalt blue features pair of plump birds perched on tree branch. Hairline crack; minor rim chip. (MARLIN G. DENLINGER AUCTION)
Excellent Quality/Excellent Condition *$450 (A)*

Six gallon A. O. Whittemore Havana, NY
Straight-sided with lug handles and single band near top. Impressed with potter's name and large numeral "6." Very unusual cobalt blue design depicting a small house above which tower a pair of tropical palm trees. (COLLECTION OF WILLARD E. GRANDE)
Superior Quality/Excellent Condition *$6,500 (D)*

Six gallon (Maker unknown)
Straight-sided with lug handles. Impressed with numeral "6." Features very large long-tailed bird rendered in cobalt blue. (MARLIN G. DENLINGER AUCTION)
Excellent Quality/Excellent Condition *$180 (A)*

Six gallon J. & E. Norton Bennington, VT
Slightly ovoid in shape with lug handles. Notable decoration in deep cobalt blue features a proud stag, a tree at each side. Some chips and obvious cracks. (COLLECTION OF WILLARD E. GRANDE)
Excellent Quality/Good Condition *$6,500 (D)*

Six gallon G. S. Guy & Co. Fort Edward, NY
Straight-sided with lug handles. Impressed with potter's name and numeral "6." Bold design in cobalt blue features plump, long-tailed bird perched on leafy branch. (MARLIN G. DENLINGER AUCTION)
Excellent Quality/Excellent Condition *$450 (A)*

Six gallon Fort Edward Stoneware Co. Fort Edward, NY
Straight-sided with lug handles. Impressed with potter's imprint and numeral "6." Unusual design in cobalt blue features a pair of crossed American flags above the date "1883." Rare. Hairline crack. (MARLIN G. DENLINGER AUCTION)
Superior Quality/Excellent Condition *$8,000 (A)*

Six gallon New York Stoneware Co. Fort Edward, NY
Straight-sided with lug handles. Impressed with maker's imprint and numeral "6." Design in cobalt blue features plump bird nesting amidst leaves and branches. Some flaking on one side and at back. (COLLECTION OF WILLARD E. GRANDE)
Excellent Quality/Good Condition *$900 (D)*

Six gallon M. Woodruff & Co. Cortland, NY
Straight-sided with lug handles and single band near top. Impressed with potter's imprint. Features almost abstract rendering in cobalt blue of bird in flight. Some kiln damage. (COLLECTION OF WILLARD E. GRANDE)
Excellent Quality/Excellent Condition *$3,000 (D)*

Six gallon Ottman Bros. & Co. Fort Edward, NY
Straight-sided with lug handles. Impressed with potter's imprint and numeral "6." Large and very bold design of plump bird seated on three-leaved branch. Some chips. (MARLIN G. DENLINGER AUCTION)
Excellent Quality/Excellent Condition *$275 (A)*

Six gallon (Maker unknown)
Straight-sided with lug handles. Simple renderings of six-petaled flower and numeral "6" in cobalt blue. Minor chips. (MARLIN G. DENLINGER AUCTION)
Excellent Quality/Excellent Condition *$100 (A)*

Six gallon (Maker unknown)
Straight-sided with lug handles. Large multileaved flower and large numeral "6" rendered in cobalt blue. Hairline crack. (MARLIN G. DENLINGER AUCTION)
Excellent Quality/Excellent Condition *$120 (A)*

Six gallon Hubbell & Chesebro Geddes, NY
Straight-sided with lug handles. Impressed with potter's mark and numeral "6." Features cheerful and distinctive floral decoration in cobalt blue. Rim chip. (COLLECTION OF WILLARD E. GRANDE)
Excellent Quality/Excellent Condition *$1,800 (D)*

Six gallon W. H. Farrar & Co. Geddes, NY
Straight-sided with lug handles. Banded near top. Impressed with potter's imprint. Numeral "6" and large floral design in cobalt blue. Chip in design. Hairline cracks at back. (ARTHUR AUCTIONEERING)
Excellent Quality/Good Condition *$200 (A)*

Twelve gallon Hamilton Pottery Greensboro, PA
Tends toward barrel shape; twenty-one and one-half inches in height. Stenciled with numeral "12" at top and bottom; also, "Hamilton's, Jones Agents, Greensboro," all enclosed within stenciled design. Hairline crack at base. (COLLECTION OF GEORGE SHAHADY)
Excellent Quality/Excellent Condition *$500 (D)*

Jars

One quart (Maker unknown)
Specifically, a canning jar. Cylinder-shaped. Decorated with three parallel strips of cobalt blue. Minor rim chip. (ARTHUR AUCTIONEERING)
Very Good Quality/Excellent Condition *$100 (A)*

One quart A. Conrad New Geneva, PA
Straight-sided canning jar. Stenciled with potter's name. Minor rim chips. (ARTHUR AUCTIONEERING)
Very Good Quality/Excellent Condition *$120 (A)*

One quart A. P. Donaghho Parkersburg, WV
Canning jar, slightly ovoid in form. Potter's name stenciled diagonally across front. Tight crack in front. (ARTHUR AUCTIONEERING)
Very Good Quality/Very Good Condition *$40 (A)*

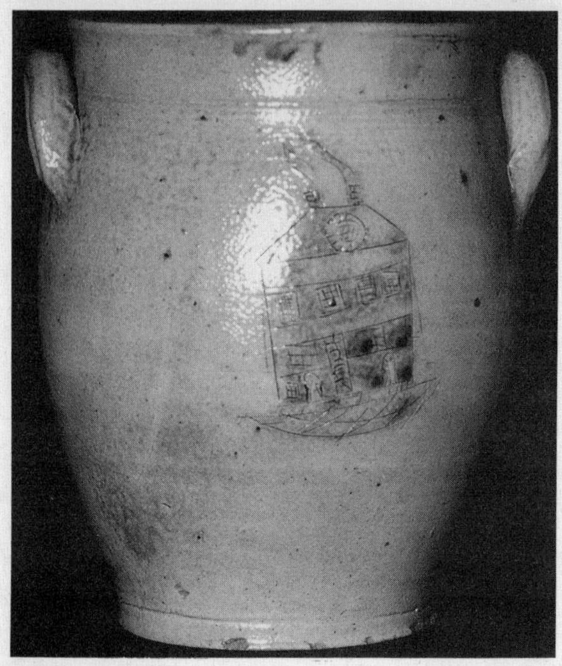

One gallon (Maker unknown)
Ovoid in shape with heavy lug handles. Very folksy decoration features incised drawing of a tall house, smoke trailing from its two chimneys, with cobalt blue adornment. Dates to early 1800s. Attributed to Hartford potter Daniel Goodale. Minor hairline cracks and small base chips. (COLLECTION OF BRAD MAXWELL)
Excellent Quality/Good Condition *$3,500 (D)*

One gallon Jas. Hamilton & Co. Greensboro, PA
Straight-sided; double-banded near top. Stenciled decoration includes potter's name and address. Minor base chips. (MARLIN G. DENLINGER AUCTION)
Excellent Quality/Excellent Condition *$110 (A)*

One gallon T. F. Reppert Greensboro, PA
Cylinder-shaped with gently sloping shoulders. Stenciled T. F. REPPERT, SUCCESSOR TO JAS. HAMILTON & CO., GREENSBORO, PA. Small stenciled floral decorations. Minor rim chip. (ARTHUR AUCTIONEERING)
Very Good Quality/Excellent Condition *$80 (A)*

One gallon (Maker unknown)
Ovoid in form with two bands near top and slightly flared mouth. Believed to be the work of Charlestown, Massachusetts, potter Frederick Carpenter. Has unusual incised and cobalt blue cross-and-swag decoration. Complete with lid. Dates to about 1810. (COLLECTION OF BRAD MAXWELL)
Excellent Quality/Good Condition *$600–$800 (D)*

One gallon F. H. Cowden Harrisburg, PA
Straight-sided with sloping shoulders. No decoration. Hairline crack at rim. (ARTHUR AUCTIONEERING)
Very Good Quality/Excellent Condition *$25 (A)*

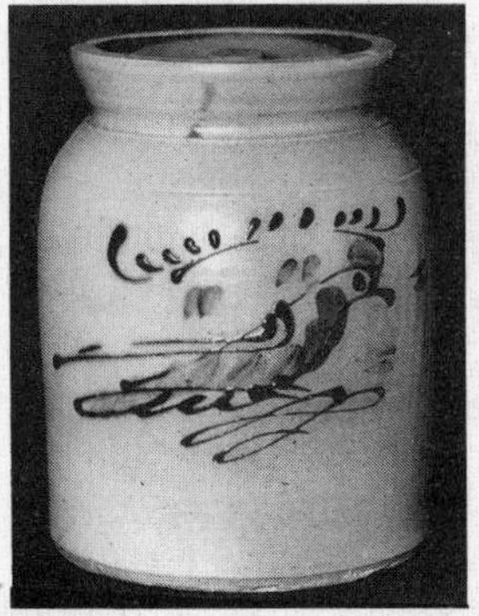

One gallon (Maker unknown)
Straight-sided with wide mouth; no handle. Design in cobalt blue features a long-billed bird perched on a tree branch. (COLLECTION OF BRAD MAXWELL)
Very Good Quality/Excellent Condition *$500–$600 (D)*

One gallon Palantine Pottery Co. Palantine, WV
Slightly bulbous. Stenciled with a picture of a pear and potter's name and address. Cracked. (ARTHUR AUCTIONEERING)
Excellent Quality/Good Condition *$100 (A)*

One gallon (Maker unknown)
Ovoid in form with lug handles. Features incised folksy rendering of man's profile, decorated in cobalt blue. Attributed to Joseph Remmey, South Amboy, New Jersey, early nineteenth century. From the collection of Georgeanna Greer. Exhibited at the San Antonio Museum of Art in 1982. Minor flaking. Very rare. (HARMER ROOKE GALLERIES)
Superior Quality/Excellent Condition *$6,250 (A)*

One gallon F. Stetzenmeyer & G. Goetzman Rochester, NY
Cylinder-shaped with slightly rounded shoulders and lug handles. Impressed with potter's imprint. Bold leaf-and-flower design rendered in cobalt blue. Hairline crack; rim chip. (MARLIN G. DENLINGER AUCTION)
Excellent Quality/Excellent Condition *$225 (A)*

One gallon Cowden & Wilcox Harrisburg, PA
Slightly bulbous with lug handles. Impressed with potter's imprint. Cobalt blue floral decoration. Blue at handles. Crack at back. (ARTHUR AUCTIONEERING)
Very Good Quality/Good Condition *$110 (A)*

One gallon Lyons
Cylinder-shaped with gently sloping shoulders and lug handles. Impressed with potter's imprint. Attractive double-flower design rendered in cobalt blue. (MARLIN G. DENLINGER AUCTION)
Excellent Quality/Fine Condition *$400 (A)*

One and one-half gallon E. & L. P. Norton Bennington, VT
Slightly bulbous in form with lug handles. With lid. Impressed with potter's imprint and "1½." Exceptional design in cobalt blue features a chicken pecking corn, only the second design of its type known to have been produced by the Norton pottery. Very rare. (COLLECTION OF BETTY AND JOEL SCHATZBERG)
Superior Quality/Excellent Condition *$15,000 (D)*

One and one-half gallon E. & P. Norton Bennington, VT
Slightly slanted sides with wide mouth and lug handles. Impressed with potter's imprint and "1½." Cobalt blue skillfully and lavishly applied to create bold floral design. Minor rim chips. (COLLECTION OF BRAD MAXWELL)
Excellent Quality/Excellent Condition *$950–$1,200 (D)*

Two gallon Martin Crafts Boston, MA
Straight-sided with gently sloping shoulders and lug handles. Impressed with potter's imprint and numeral "2." Bold and elaborate design in dark cobalt blue. (MARLIN G. DENLINGER AUCTION)
Excellent Quality/Fine Condition *$725 (A)*

Six quart (Maker unknown)
Cylinder-shaped with sloping shoulders and flared mouth. Classified as a cookie jar. Impressed with large numeral "6" and user's mark—WALKER & CO., 27 HAVERHILL ST., BOSTON, MASS. Elaborately decorated in dark cobalt blue. Scene depicts a large bird in a small, tilted tree. Probably made in Fort Edward, New York. (COLLECTION OF WILLIAM E. GRANDE)
Excellent Quality/Excellent Condition *$2,800 (D)*

Two gallon N. Clark, Jr. Athens, NY
Cylinder-shaped with rounded shoulders and lug handles. Impressed with potter's name and numeral "2." Design in cobalt blue features plump bird perched on small branch. Chip at handle. (MARLIN G. DENLINGER AUCTION)
Excellent Quality/Excellent Condition *$450 (A)*

Two gallon (Maker unknown)
Squat preserve jar with interior brown slip glaze. Decorated in cobalt blue slip with large "2" and simple calligraphic design. Attributed to Denton County, Texas, pottery, 1860–1870. Pictured in *American Stonewares*. From the collection of Georgeanna Greer. Unusual. (HARMER ROOKE GALLERIES)
Excellent Quality/Excellent Condition *$550 (A)*

Two gallon J. & N. Norton Bennington, VT
Slightly sloping sides and lug handles. Impressed with maker's mark and numeral "2." Features dark and heavily glazed cobalt blue rendering of a long-tailed bird. Kiln burn near bird's head. (COLLECTION OF BRAD MAXWELL)
Excellent Quality/Good Condition *$1,500–$2,000 (D)*

Two gallon Harrington & Burger Rochester, NY
Straight-sided with rounded shoulders and lug handles. Impressed with maker's imprint. With lid. Bold floral decoration and numeral "2" in cobalt blue. Minor chips. (ARTHUR AUCTIONEERING)
Excellent Quality/Excellent Condition *$375 (A)*

Two gallon John Burger Rochester, NY
Cylinder-shaped with slightly rounded shoulders and lug handles. Impressed with potter's imprint. Double-leaf design and numeral "2" rendered in cobalt blue. Crack at back; rim chip. (MARLIN G. DENLINGER AUCTION)
Excellent Quality/Very Good Condition *$110 (A)*

Two gallon (Maker unknown)
Straight-sided. No handles. Cobalt blue floral decoration at front. Some chips. (ARTHUR AUCTIONEERING)
Good Quality/Excellent Condition *$150 (A)*

Two gallon Burger & Lang Rochester, NY
Cylinder-shaped with slightly rounded shoulders and lug handles. Impressed with potter's imprint. Leafy tulip and numeral "2" rendered in cobalt blue. (MARLIN G. DENLINGER AUCTION)
Excellent Quality/Excellent Condition *$250 (A)*

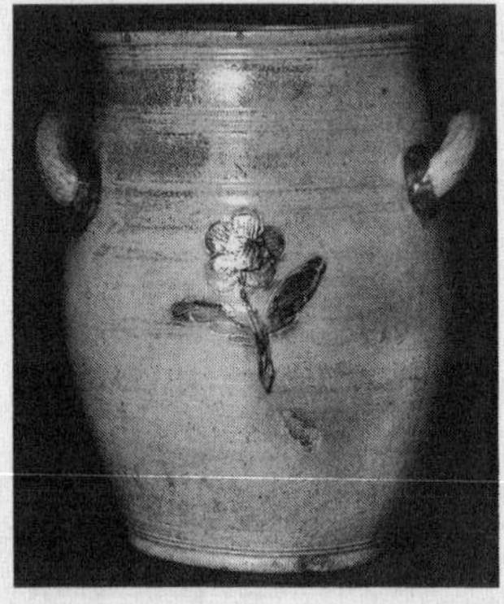

Two gallon (Maker unknown)
Slightly ovoid in shape with free-standing handles. Classified as a cream pot. Incised floral design decorated in cobalt blue at front and back. Believed to be the work of Jonathan Fenton. (COLLECTION OF BRAD MAXWELL)
Excellent Quality/Excellent Condition *$1,800–$2,000 (D)*

Two gallon (Maker unknown)
Cylinder-shaped with gently sloping shoulders. Encircled at top with leaf designs in cobalt blue. (MARLIN G. DENLINGER AUCTION)
Excellent Quality/Excellent Condition *$170 (A)*

Two gallon H. Wilson & Co. Guadalupe, TX
Cylinder-shaped with rounded shoulders. Impressed with large numeral "2" and maker's name. Dates from 1870 to 1884. From the collection of Georgeanna Greer. (HARMER ROOKE GALLERIES)
Excellent Quality/Excellent Condition *$475 (A)*

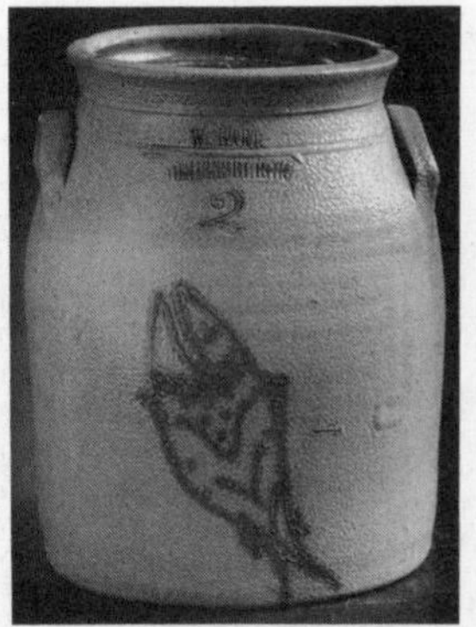

Two gallon W. Hart Ogdensburgh, NY
Lug handles; two bands near top. Impressed with potter's mark and numeral "3." Features cobalt blue design of fish, almost vertical (apparently swimming toward the surface). Some chips on rim and one handle; minor flaking. (COLLECTION OF WILLARD E. GRANDE)
Very Good Quality/Good Condition *$2,800 (D)*

Two gallon Fenton & Hancock St. Johnsbury, VT
Slightly bulbous with lug handles. Impressed with potter's imprint and numeral "2." Bold leafy design rendered in cobalt blue. (MARLIN G. DENLINGER AUCTION)
Excellent Quality/Excellent Condition *$225 (A)*

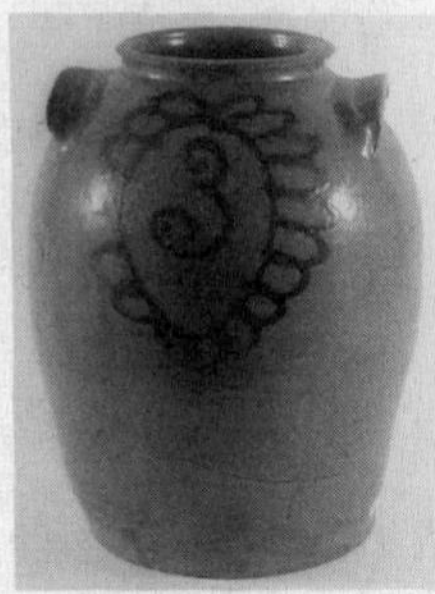

Three gallon (Maker unknown)
Somewhat ovoid in shape with ash glaze and lug handles. Decorated on front and back with large brown "3" enclosed in an oval-shaped design made up of overlapping loops. Small rim chip. Probably from the Trapp-Chandler site, South Carolina. Dates to about 1850. From the collection of Georgeanna Greer. (HARMER ROOKE GALLERIES)
Excellent Quality/Excellent Condition *$1,600 (A)*

Three gallon Ottman Brothers Fort Edward, NY
Cylinder-shaped with narrow shoulders and lug handles. Impressed with maker's mark and large numeral "3." Produced in honor of nation's centennial, design features "1876" enclosed in a leafy wreath. Scarce. (COLLECTION OF WILLARD E. GRANDE)
Excellent Quality/Excellent Condition *$550 (D)*

Three gallon White's Utica, NY
Cylinder-shaped with slightly rounded shoulders and lug handles. Impressed with maker's mark. Elaborate leaf-and-flower design rendered in cobalt blue. (MARLIN G. DENLINGER AUCTION)
Excellent Quality/Excellent Condition *$350 (A)*

Three gallon Commeraw NY City
Ovoid in shape with loop handles. Features incised swag-and-tassel design in cobalt blue that encircles the piece below the handles. Bears potter's imprint COMMERAWS STONEWARE (with several letters reversed) on one side; N. YORK CORLEARS HOOK is imprinted on other side. Dates to around 1800. From the collection of Georgeanna Greer. Very rare. (HARMER ROOKE GALLERIES)
Superior Quality/Excellent Condition *$3,750 (A)*

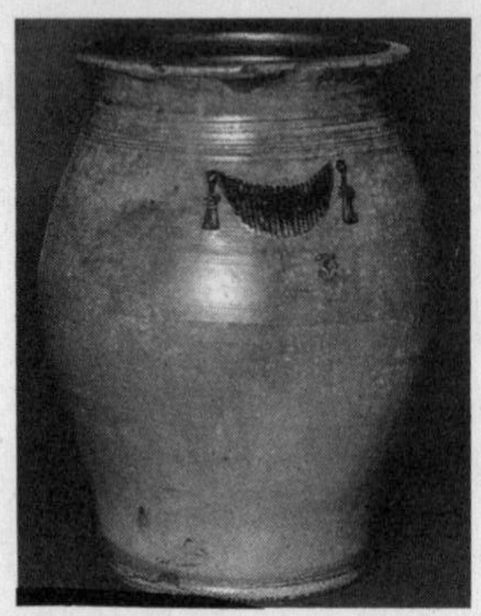

Three gallon (Maker unknown)
Wide-mouthed, slightly ovoid in form. Incised swag-and-tassel decoration finished in cobalt blue at front and back. Some rim chips. Dates to about 1810. Believed to be the work of Frederick Carpenter of Charlestown, Massachusetts. (COLLECTION OF BRAD MAXWELL)
Excellent Quality/Very Good Condition *$650–$800 (D)*

Three gallon (Maker unknown)
Ovoid in shape with dark olive-brown glaze. Lug handles. Decorated with eight-petaled flower in brown slip, outlined in white slip. Some small rim chips. Attributed to Collin Rhodes, Edgefield, South Carolina. Dates to about 1840. From the collection of Georgeanna Greer. Very rare. (HARMER ROOKE GALLERIES)
Superior Quality/Excellent Condition *$2,600 (A)*

Three gallon (Maker unknown)
Ovoid in form with lug handles. Bands of ocher dip at top and bottom, creating wide light band about the piece's belly. BOSTON and "1804" impressed near top on both sides. Produced by Charlestown, Massachusetts, potter Frederick Carpenter. Minor kiln damage. (COLLECTION OF BRAD MAXWELL)
Excellent Quality/Good Condition *$1,500–$2,000 (D)*

Three gallon New York Stoneware Co. Fort Edward, NY
Cylinder-shaped with sloping shoulders and lug handles. Impressed with potter's imprint and numeral "3." Decorated in cobalt blue with rendering of a bush-tailed chicken pecking at feed. Minor rim chips. (ARTHUR AUCTIONEERING)
Excellent Quality/Excellent Condition *$1,200 (A)*

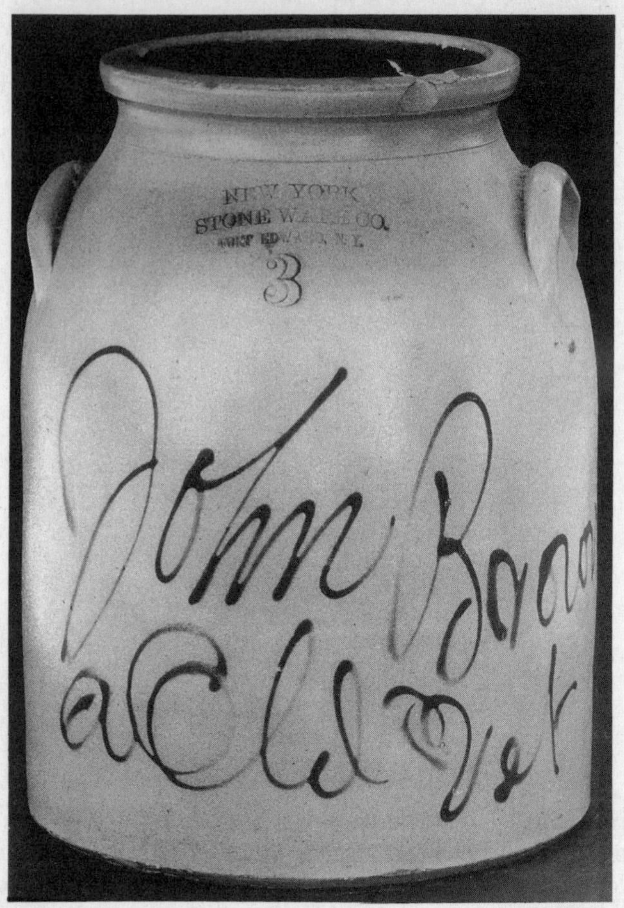

Three gallon New York Stoneware Co. Fort Edward, NY
Wide-mouthed with lug handles. Impressed with potter's name and numeral "3." Scrawled in cobalt blue across the front are the words "John Brown, a [*sic*] Old Vet." Minor rim chips. (COLLECTION OF JACK AND PAT MCMACKIN)
Excellent Quality/Excellent Condition *$2,500–$3,000 (D)*

Three gallon Cowden & Wilcox Harrisburg, PA
Straight-sided with lug handles. Impressed with potter's imprint. Bold floral design in cobalt blue and blue at handles. (ARTHUR AUCTIONEERING)
Excellent Quality/Excellent Condition *$600 (A)*

Three gallon (Maker unknown)
Ovoid in form with free-standing handles. BOSTON impressed on each side. Also features incised codfish on each side, decorated in cobalt blue. From Boston pottery of Jonathan Fenton. Base chip. (LITCHFIELD AUCTION GALLERY)
Excellent Quality/Excellent Condition *$3,500–$4,000 (D)*

Four gallon J. & E. Norton Bennington, VT
Cylinder-shaped with rounded shoulders and lug handles. Impressed with potter's imprint and large numeral "4." Very large and unusual design in cobalt blue features pair of birds, their long tails crossing, perched on a tree stump. Important. Chip on handle; hairline crack. (MARLIN G. DENLINGER AUCTION)
Superior Quality/Excellent Condition *$3,000 (A)*

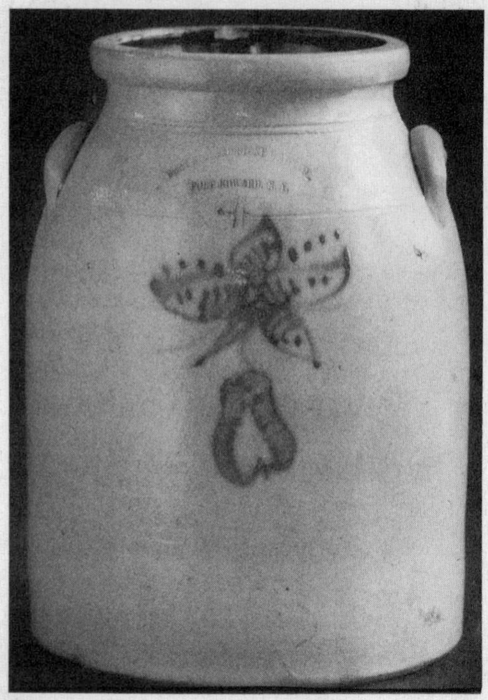

Four gallon Fort Edward Stoneware Co. Fort Edward, NY
Straight-sided with sloping shoulders and lug handles. Impressed with potter's imprint and large numeral "4." Decoration in cobalt blue pictures a sprig of leaves and a single pear dangling from it. Dates from 1875 to 1882. (COLLECTION OF WILLARD E. GRANDE)
Very Good Quality/Excellent Condition *$650 (D)*

Four gallon J. & E. Norton Bennington, VT
Cylinder-shaped with rounded shoulders and lug handles. Impressed with potter's imprint and large numeral "4." Large and vivid design in cobalt blue features reclining stag between two rail fences. Hairline crack. (MARLIN DENLINGER AUCTION)
Superior Quality/Excellent Condition *$3,300 (A)*

Five gallon (Maker unknown)
Slightly slanted sides with lug handles. From western Pennsylvania. Free-hand floral decorations at both front and back, plus large free-hand numeral "5." (ARTHUR AUCTIONEERING)
Excellent Quality/Excellent Condition *$450 (A)*

Five gallon Louis Miles Edgefield, SC

Ovoid in form with deep olive-green mottled glaze. Lug handles. Incised in script: LM DAVE JAN 29, 1859. (Dave was a slave who belonged to Miles and worked at the pottery.) Two vertical hairline cracks, each several inches in length. Very rare. (HARMER ROOKE GALLERIES)

Superior Quality/Excellent Condition *$6,750 (A)*

Five gallon James Hamilton & Co. Greensboro, PA

Slanted sides with lug handles. Stenciled with potter's name and address, numeral "5," and several floral designs. (ARTHUR AUCTIONEERING)

Excellent Quality/Excellent Condition *$400 (A)*

Six gallon White's Utica, NY
Slightly ovoid in shape with lug handles. Impressed with potter's imprint and numeral "6." Bold design in cobalt blue features pair of birds facing each other while perched on flowered branch. Hairline crack. (MARLIN G. DENLINGER AUCTION)
Excellent Quality/Excellent Condition *$360 (A)*

Six gallon (Maker unknown)
Somewhat ovoid in form with brown alkaline glaze. Inscribed with large numeral "6." Attributed to Rusk County, Texas. Dates to about 1870. Interesting bubbly surface. Hairline crack and some bubble bursts. From the collection of Georgeanna Greer. (HARMER ROOKE GALLERIES)
Excellent Quality/Excellent Condition *$475 (A)*

Six gallon Williams & Reppert Greensboro, PA
Slightly slanted sides with lug handles. Stenciled with potter's name. Stenciled and free-hand decoration. (ARTHUR AUCTIONEERING)
Excellent Quality/Very Good Condition *$400 (A)*

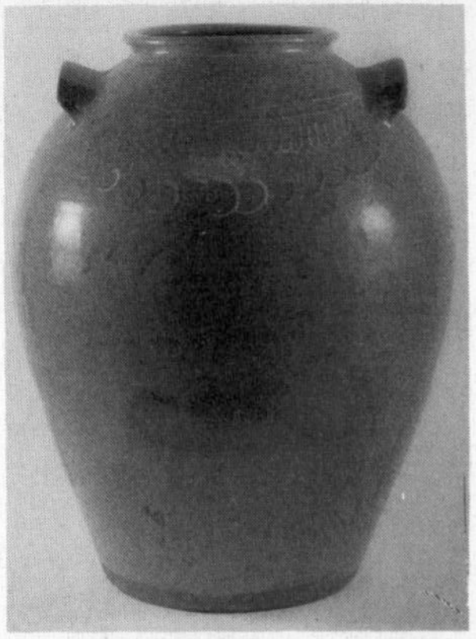

Ten gallon Thomas Chandler Edgefield, SC
Ovoid in form with light green alkaline glaze. Lug handles. Features loop-and-swag decoration that encircles piece beneath handles and, just below, an open loop design. CHANDLER MAKER impressed on one side near top. Dates to about 1850. Several hairline cracks. Rare and important. (HARMER ROOKE GALLERIES)
Superior Quality/Excellent Condition *$3,600 (A)*

(Capacity unknown) (Maker unknown)
Unusual leech jar (for storage of freshwater leeches, formerly used in medicine for bloodletting). Takes the form of a squat jug that has been pierced with several hundred pencil-size holes. Scarce. (COLLECTION OF TRACY LAW)
Excellent Quality/Excellent Condition *$650 (D)*

Jugs

One quart N. Fox NC
Ovoid in shape with brown glaze and strap handle. Impressed with potter's name. Dates from 1850 to 1870. (HARMER ROOKE GALLERIES)
Excellent Quality/Excellent Condition *$600 (A)*

One-half gallon Thomas Commeraw NY City
Straight-sided, rounded at the shoulder. Crudely impressed with the name COMMERAW and the word STONEWARE (with a backward N). Also bears unusual incised clamshell design on front and back. Believed to date to 1802. Very scarce. (COLLECTION OF BRAD MAXWELL)
Superior Quality/Excellent Condition *$3,000–$4,000 (D)*

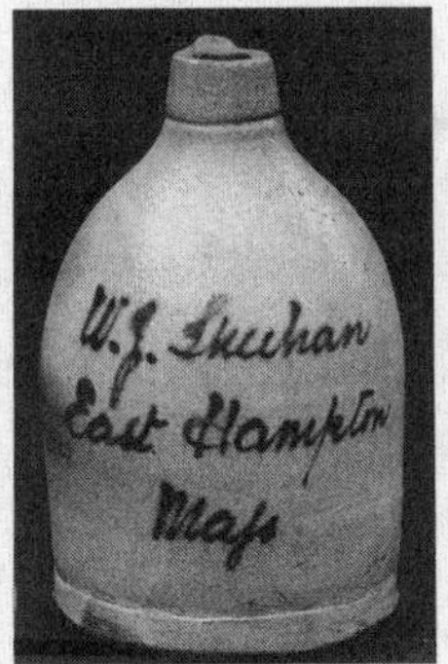

One-half gallon (Maker unknown)
Typical shoulder jug with strap handle. Typical of Albany-area potters during latter half of nineteenth century. Blazoned in cobalt blue script with the name "W. J. Sheehan, East Hampton, Mass." Minor chips at mouth. (COLLECTION OF BILL SULLIVAN)
Very Good Quality/Excellent Condition *$150 (A)*

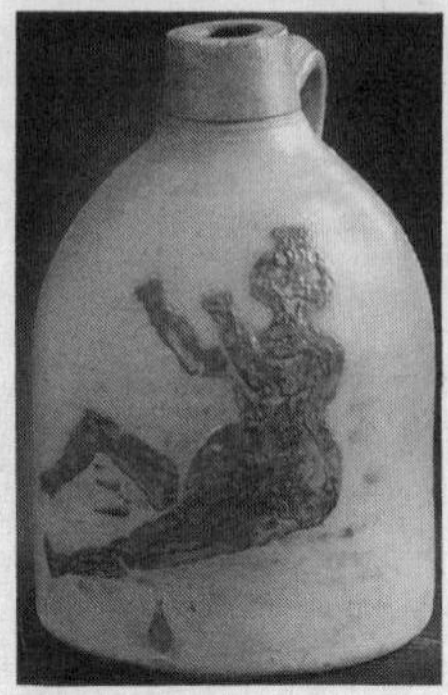

One-half gallon (Maker unknown)
Cylinder-shaped with rounded shoulders and strap handle. Notable for its bizarre cobalt blue decorations—a pregnant woman seated on the ground, her fists clenched, her arms upraised. Dates to latter decades of the nineteenth century. Rim chip. (COLLECTION OF WILLARD E. GRANDE)
Excellent Quality/Excellent Condition *$2,400 (D)*

One-half gallon (Maker unknown)
Grotesque face jug in straw-colored alkaline glaze. Strap handle. Pupils of eyes rendered in cobalt blue. Teeth made of ironstone strands. From northern Mississippi, late nineteenth century. Exhibited at Mississippi State Museum, 1980. From the collection of Georgeanna Greer. (HARMER ROOKE GALLERIES)
Superior Quality/Excellent Condition *$5,500 (A)*

One-half gallon (Maker unknown)
Cylinder-shaped with rounded shoulders and strap handle. Simple swirl rendered in cobalt blue. Hairline crack. (MARLIN G. DENLINGER AUCTION)
Very Good Quality/Excellent Condition *$70 (A)*

One gallon (Maker unknown)
Ovoid in form with loop handle. Classified as a whiskey jug. Features incised cartouche at front with initials "J.F." in fancy script, decorated in cobalt blue. BOSTON impressed on opposite side. Chip at lip and hairline crack in handle. Attributed to Jonathan Fenton. From the collection of Georgeanna Greer. Exhibited at San Antonio Museum of Art in 1982. Rare. (HARMER ROOKE GALLERIES)
Superior Quality/Excellent Condition *$3,000 (A)*

One gallon Jonathan Fenton
Brown-glazed and classically ovoid in form. J. FENTON impressed near top. Bears incised design of fish decorated in cobalt blue. Attractive banding near top and at shoulders. Dates to 1804. Very rare. Some kiln damage. (COLLECTION OF BRAD MAXWELL)
Excellent Quality/Excellent Condition *$2,500–$3,200 (D)*

One gallon C. Crolius NY City
Ovoid in shape with cobalt blue scallop decoration near top. Imprinted with potter's name: C. CROLIUS MANUFACTURER NEW YORK. Classified as a whiskey jug. From the collection of Georgeanna Greer. Minor flaking. Rare. (HARMER ROOKE GALLERIES)
Superior Quality/Very Good Condition *$850 (A)*

One gallon New York Stoneware Co. Fort Edward, NY
Slightly squatty in shape with sloping shoulders and strap handle. Impressed with potter's imprint. Bold design in cobalt blue of bird perched on leafy branch. Small hole drilled at back. (MARLIN G. DENLINGER AUCTION)
Excellent Quality/Very Good Condition *$300 (A)*

One gallon (Maker unknown)
Somewhat ovoid in form with runny olive-green ash glaze. From Crawford County, Georgia. Dates from 1860 to 1870. From the collection of Georgeanna Greer. (HARMER ROOKE GALLERIES)
Excellent Quality/Excellent Condition *$100 (A)*

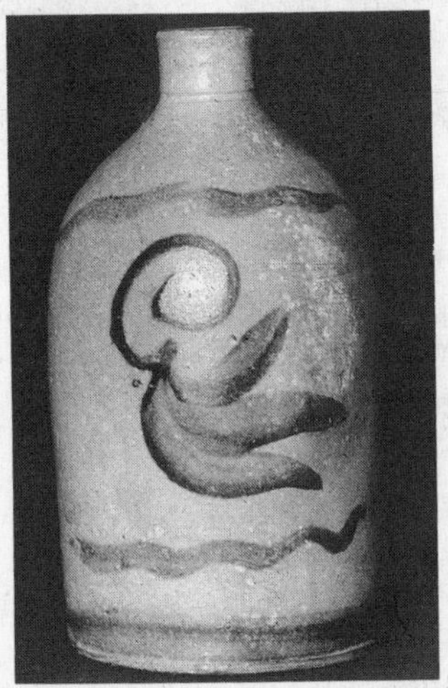

One gallon (Maker unknown)
Cylinder-shaped with rounded shoulders and strap handle. Cheerful floral decoration in cobalt blue. The work of an unidentified Pennsylvania potter. Dates to about 1840. (COLLECTION OF BRAD MAXWELL)
Excellent Quality/Excellent Condition *$300–$450 (D)*

One gallon (Maker unknown)
Grotesque face jug in dark brown glaze. From southern United States, dating to around 1900. From the collection of Georgeanna Greer. Unique. (HARMER ROOKE GALLERIES)
Superior Quality/Excellent Condition *$1,500 (A)*

One gallon N. White & Co. Binghamton, NY
Cylinder-shaped with rounded shoulders and strap handle. Impressed with potter's name. Design features bird perched on branch in cobalt blue. (MARLIN G. DENLINGER AUCTION)
Very Good Quality/Fine Condition *$170 (A)*

One gallon (Maker unknown)
Squatty in form with strap handle. Blazoned with owner's name and address in cobalt blue script: "B. Feiock & Co., Rochester, N.Y." (MARLIN G. DENLINGER AUCTION)
Very Good Quality/Excellent Condition *$100 (A)*

One gallon Ham Brothers
Squat whiskey jug with a strap handle. Impressed with potter's imprint. From the collection of Georgeanna Greer. A classic. (HARMER ROOKE GALLERIES)
Excellent Quality/Excellent Condition *$110 (A)*

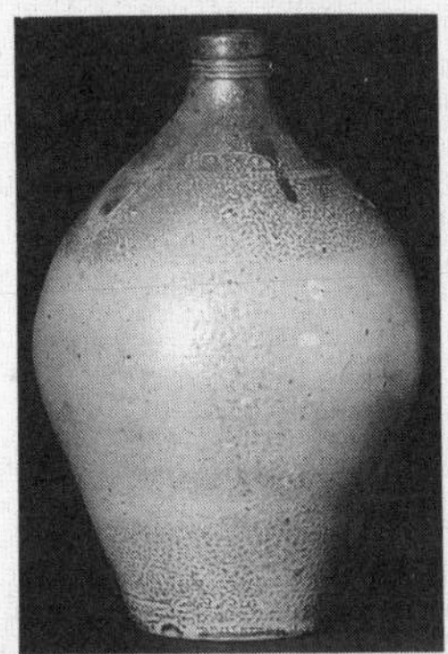

One gallon (Maker unknown)
Ovoid in form with attractive coggled band below neck. BOSTON impressed just above band. Ocher dipped at top and bottom. Attributed to Charlestown, Massachusetts, potter Frederick Carpenter. Dates to about 1810. (COLLECTION OF BRAD MAXWELL)
Excellent Quality/Excellent Condition *$175–$275 (D)*

One gallon Haxstun, Ottman & Co. Fort Edward, NY
Cylinder-shaped with rounded shoulders and strap handle. Impressed with potter's imprint. Rendering in cobalt blue of big-billed bird on a leafy branch. Minor rim chip. (MARLIN G. DENLINGER AUCTION)
Excellent Quality/Excellent Condition *$375 (A)*

One gallon Tyler & Dillon Albany, NY
Ovoid in form with strap handle. Impressed with potter's imprint. Large numeral "1" in cobalt blue. (ARTHUR AUCTIONEERING)
Very Good Quality/Excellent Condition *$130 (A)*

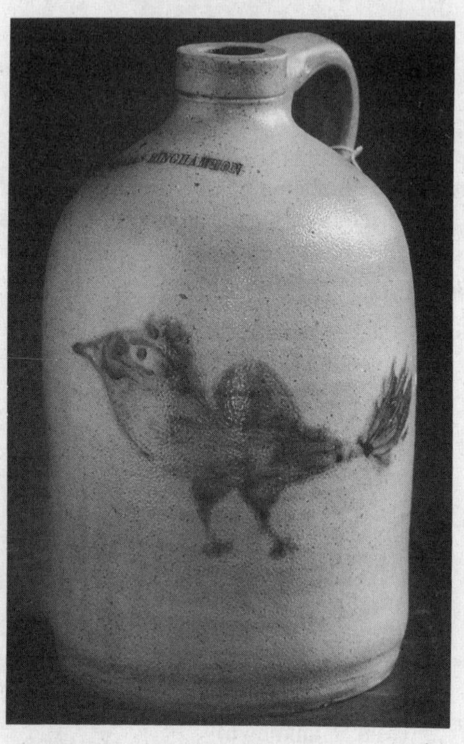

One gallon White Binghamton, NY
Straight-sided shouldered jug with strap handle. Bears imprint WHITE'S BINGHAMTON. Decorated in cobalt blue with a fanciful creature, part fowl, part fish. Interesting. Dates from 1849 to 1866. (COLLECTION OF WILLARD E. GRANDE)
Excellent Quality/Excellent Condition *$1,400 (D)*

One gallon N. Clark, Jr. Athens, NY
Cylinder-shaped with rounded shoulders. Impressed with potter's imprint. Fancy floral design rendered in cobalt blue. (MARLIN G. DENLINGER AUCTION)
Excellent Quality/Excellent Condition *$225 (A)*

One gallon (Maker unknown)
Cylinder-shaped with rounded shoulders and strap handle. Blazoned with "R. M. & Co., Troy" in cobalt blue script. (MARLIN G. DENLINGER AUCTION)
Excellent Quality/Excellent Condition *$80 (A)*

One gallon Thomas Commeraw NY City
Ovoid in shape, ocher in color. Incised with double clamshell design, finished in cobalt blue. Bears potter's name and address: "COMMERAW STONEWARE, CORLEARS HOOK, N. YORK," printed in five-line arrangement. Very rare. (COLLECTION OF BRAD MAXWELL)
Superior Quality/Excellent Condition *$3,500–$4,000 (D)*

One gallon Ottman Brothers & Co. Fort Edward, NY
Cylinder-shaped with rounded shoulders and strap handle. Impressed with potter's imprint. Bold double-flower design rendered in cobalt blue. Minor rim chip. (MARLIN G. DENLINGER AUCTION)
Excellent Quality/Excellent Condition *$160 (A)*

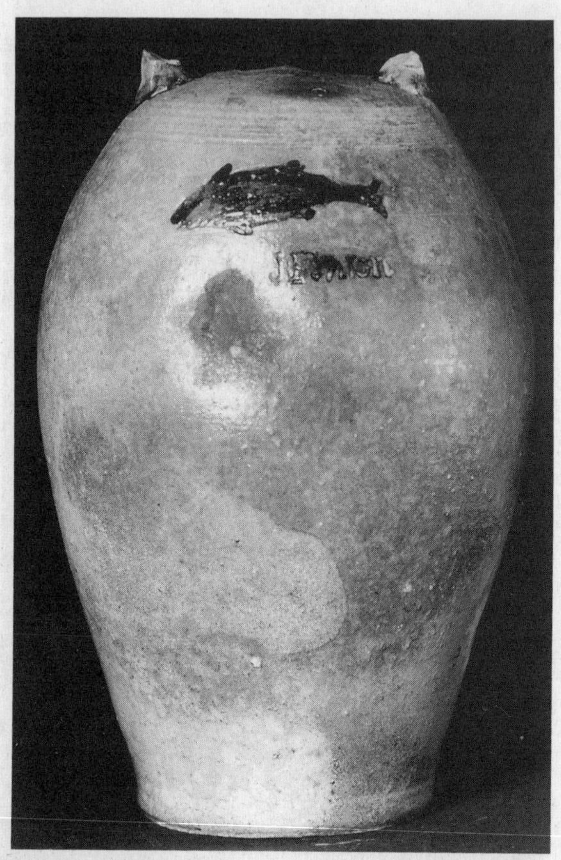

One and one-half gallon Jonathan Fenton
One of the earliest field jugs known. Tall and ovoid in form and coated in brown glaze. Impressed with potter's name—J. FENTON. Design features an incised fish decorated in cobalt blue. Very rare; one of a kind. Some kiln damage. Handle missing. (COLLECTION OF BRAD MAXWELL)
Excellent Quality/Good Condition *$2,000–$3,000 (D)*

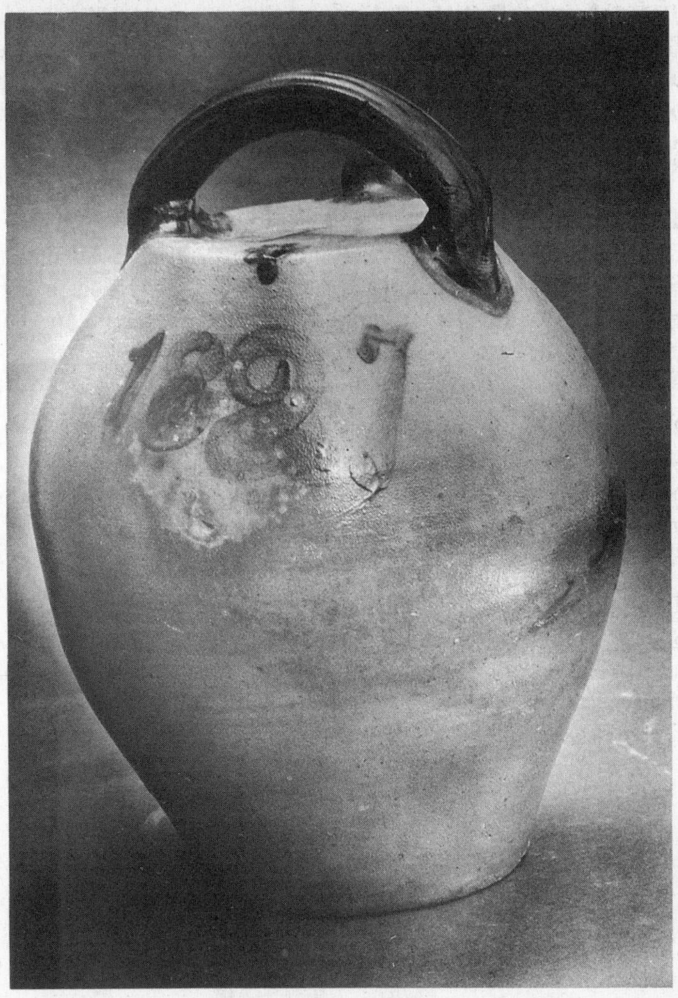

Two gallon (Maker unknown)
Ovoid in form with heavy bail handle across the top. Known specifically as a harvest jug. Two spouts at top—one for drinking, the other for filling or pouring. Blazoned with "1827" in cobalt blue. Believed to have been produced in western Pennsylvania. Very rare. Some kiln damage. (COLLECTION OF BETTY AND JOEL SCHATZBERG)
Superior Quality/Excellent Condition *$15,000–$20,000 (D)*

Two gallon E. & L. P. Norton Bennington, VT
Cylinder-shaped with rounded shoulders. Impressed with potter's name and numeral "2." Cobalt blue rendering of a long-tailed bird perched on a leafy branch. Hairline crack. (MARLIN G. DENLINGER AUCTION)
Excellent Quality/Excellent Condition *$450 (A)*

Two gallon N. Clark, Jr. Athens, NY
Cylinder-shaped with rounded shoulders and strap handle. Impressed with potter's mark and numeral "2." Blazoned in cobalt blue with double-flower, double-leaf design. Crack in back. (MARLIN G. DENLINGER AUCTION)
Excellent Quality/Good Condition *$95 (A)*

Two gallon A. O. Whittemore Havana, NY
Squatty with rounded shoulders and strap handle. Impressed with potter's imprint. Decorated in cobalt blue with floral design and numeral "2." Minor rim chip. (MARLIN G. DENLINGER AUCTION)
Excellent Quality/Excellent Condition *$100 (A)*

Two gallon A. O. Whittemore Havana, NY
Squatty with strap handle. Impressed with potter's imprint and numeral "2." Decorated in cobalt blue with strutting bird. Minor base chips; some flaking. (ARTHUR AUCTIONEERING)
Excellent Quality/Good Condition *$250 (A)*

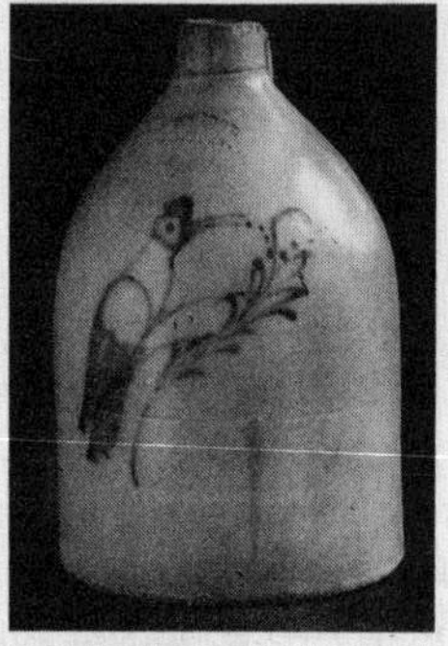

Two gallon West Troy Pottery West Troy, NY
Impressed with potter's mark and the numeral "2." Features bold depiction of long-billed bird perched on the branch of a berry tree eating the fruit. Rim chips. (COLLECTION OF WILLARD E. GRANDE)
Excellent Quality/Good Condition *$475 (D)*

Two gallon West Troy Pottery West Troy, NY
Cylinder-shaped with rounded shoulders and strap handle. Impressed with potter's imprint. Bold double-flower design rendered in cobalt blue. Minor rim chip. (MARLIN G. DENLINGER AUCTION)
Excellent Quality/Excellent Condition *$160 (A)*

Two gallon Thomas Ownby Union County, SC
Ovoid in form with deep olive-green alkaline glaze. Strap handle. Inscribed by hand: "August the 30 / 1864 / maid and sold at / a low price for confederat / money by me / Thomas Ownbey." Pictured in *American Stonewares*. From the collection of Georgeanna Greer. Very rare. (HARMER ROOKE GALLERIES)
Superior Quality/Excellent Condition *$16,500 (A)*

Two gallon F. H. Cowden Harrisburg, PA
Cylinder-shaped with rounded shoulders and strap handle. Impressed with potter's name. Decorated with large and handsome stenciled snowflake. Minor base chips. (MARLIN G. DENLINGER AUCTION)
Excellent Quality/Excellent Condition *$110 (A)*

Two gallon J. & E. Norton Bennington, VT
Cylinder-shaped with sloping shoulders and strap handle. Impressed with potter's imprint. Large, bold floral design in cobalt blue. Small base chip and hairline crack. (COLLECTION OF WILLARD E. GRANDE)
Excellent Quality/Excellent Condition *$400 (D)*

Two gallon C. L. Williams & Co. Geneva, PA
Slightly bulbous. Strap handle missing. Stenciled C. L. WILLIAMS & CO., BEST BLUE STONEWARE, GENEVA, PA. (ARTHUR AUCTIONEERING)
Good Quality/Poor Condition *$100 (A)*

Two gallon (Maker unknown)
Cylinder-shaped with rounded shoulders and single strap handle. J. & E. Norton of Bennington, Vermont, is believed to have produced the piece, although it is impressed with the name of a Boston wine merchant—E. H. MAXWELL, 79 & 81 BROAD ST., BOSTON, and a large numeral "2." Depicts skillfully drawn stags in resting position. (COLLECTION OF WILLARD E. GRANDE)
Excellent Quality/Good Condition *$5,500 (D)*

Two gallon A. K. Ballard Burlington, VT
Cylinder-shaped with rounded shoulders and strap handle. Impressed with potter's mark and numeral "2." Small cobalt blue floral decoration. Minor rim chip. (ARTHUR AUCTIONEERING)
Very Good Quality/Excellent Condition *$110 (A)*

Two gallon J. & E. Norton Bennington, VT
Cylinder-shaped with rounded shoulders and strap handle. Impressed with maker's mark. Features stately game bird perched on gaily flowered branch. Rare. (COLLECTION OF BETTY AND JOEL SCHATZBERG)
Excellent Quality/Excellent Condition *$15,000 (D)*

Two gallon Burger & Lang Rochester, NY
Slightly ovoid in shape with strap handle. Impressed with maker's imprint. Numeral "2" enclosed in leafy wreath rendered in cobalt blue. Rim chip. (MARLIN G. DENLINGER AUCTION)
Excellent Quality/Excellent Condition *$110 (A)*

Two gallon J. & E. Norton Bennington, NY
Cylinder-shaped with sloping shoulders and strap handle. Impressed with potter's name and numeral "2." Handsome, long-tailed bird perched on branch rendered in cobalt blue. (MARLIN G. DENLINGER AUCTION)
Excellent Quality/Excellent Condition *$650 (A)*

Two gallon Cowden & Wilcox Harrisburg, PA
Ovoid in form with strap handle. Impressed with potter's imprint. Decorated in cobalt blue with unusual man-in-the-moon drawing. (ARTHUR AUCTIONEERING)
Superior Quality/Excellent Condition *$4,000 (A)*

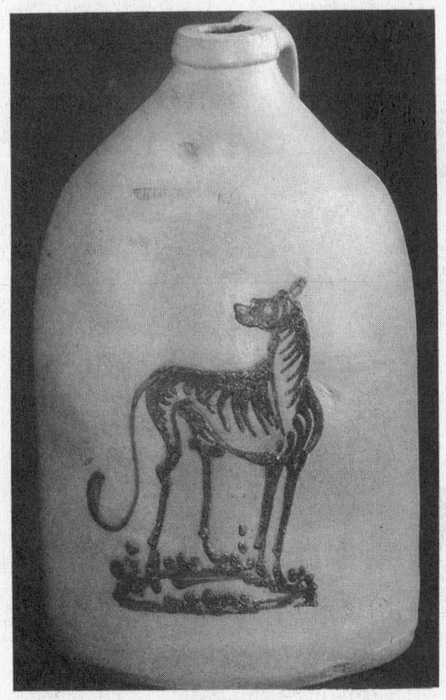

Two gallon White's Utica, NY
Cylinder-shaped with sloping shoulders and strap handle. Impressed with maker's mark and numeral "2." Design in cobalt blue features a curious-looking dog—a Great Dane, perhaps—with a long curly tail. Dates from 1849 to 1877. Unusual. Some kiln damage. (COLLECTION OF WILLARD E. GRANDE)
Excellent Quality/Excellent Condition *$4,800 (D)*

Two gallon (Maker unknown)
Ovoid in form with strap handle. CLEAN, NY impressed near top. Fernlike decoration and large numeral "2" in cobalt blue. (ARTHUR AUCTIONEERING)
Excellent Quality/Excellent Condition *$200 (A)*

Two gallon Barnabus Edmonds Charlestown, MA
Ovoid in shape with strap handle. Striking incised design, decorated in cobalt blue, features American eagle within a frame of draped tassled cord. Also impresssed with potter's imprint and a fish-and-leaf design. Dates to about 1840. Pictured on jacket of *American Stonewares*. From the collection of Georgeanna Greer. Few hairline cracks. Outstanding. (HARMER ROOKE GALLERIES)
Superior Quality/Excellent Condition *$15,500 (A)*

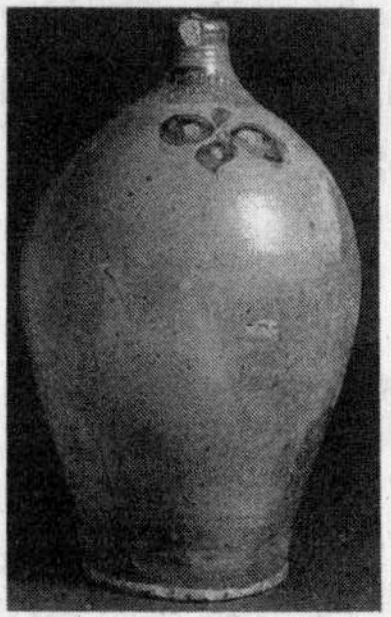

Two gallon Peter Cross Hartford, CT
Tall and ovoid in form with strap handle. Impressed P. CROSS and HARTFORD near mouth. Small incised and cobalt-decorated floral design. Cracks and chips. (LITCHFIELD AUCTION GALLERY)
Excellent Quality/Good Condition *$650 (A)*

Two gallon White's Utica, NY
Cylinder-shaped with sloping shoulders and strap handle. Impressed with potter's imprint. Decorated with large floral design and stenciled JOHN COYNE, UTICA, N.Y. in cobalt blue. (MARLIN G. DENLINGER AUCTION)
Excellent Quality/Excellent Condition *$150 (A)*

Two gallon (Maker unknown)
Squat ovoid in form, with threaded neck. Design includes coggled crosses and impressed word CHARLETSTOWN [*sic*]. Perhaps produced by the Edmands Pottery of Charlestown, Massachusetts. Quarter-size body chip. (LITCHFIELD AUCTION GALLERY)
Excellent Quality/Good Condition *$1,000–$1,250 (D)*

Two gallon A. J. Butler & Co. New Brunswick, NJ
Squatty with strap handle. Impressed with potter's imprint. Decorated in cobalt blue with large numeral "2." Rim chip, age lines. (ARTHUR AUCTIONEERING)
Very Good Quality/Very Good Condition *$80 (A)*

Two gallon Frank B. Norton Co. Worcester, MA
Wide-mouthed. Impressed with potter's imprint below numeral "2." Bold cobalt blue design featuring parrot—the "Worcester parrot"—perched on a heavily leafed branch. (COLLECTION OF BRAD MAXWELL)
Very Good Quality/Excellent Condition *$950–$1,400 (D)*

Two gallon I. M. Mead Mogadore, OH
Ovoid in form with strap handle. Impressed with potter's name. Simple floral decoration in cobalt blue. (ARTHUR AUCTIONEERING)
Very Good Quality/Excellent Condition *$325 (A)*

Two gallon A. O. Whittemore Havana, NY
Somewhat squatty with rounded shoulders and strap handle. Impressed with potter's imprint and numeral "2." Design in cobalt blue features bushy-tailed bird on leafy branch. (MARLIN G. DENLINGER AUCTION)
Excellent Quality/Excellent Condition *$400 (A)*

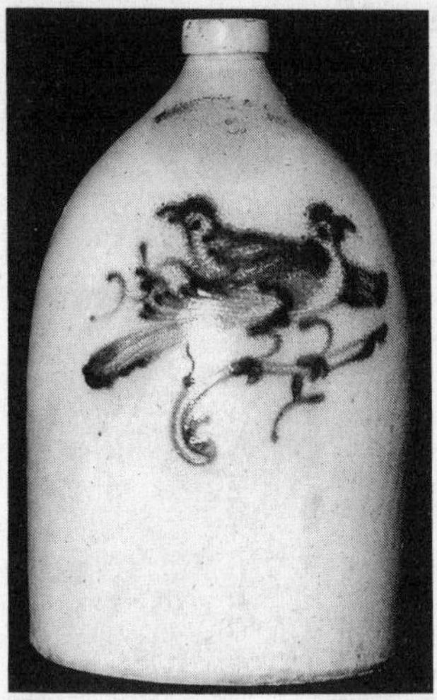

Two gallon J. Norton & Co. Bennington, VT
Shouldered jug with strap handle. Impressed with potter's name and numeral "3." Conventional cobalt blue bird design. (COLLECTION OF BRAD MAXWELL)
Excellent Quality/Fine Condition *$1,800–$2,000 (D)*

Two gallon (Maker unknown)
Cylinder-shaped with rounded shoulders. Wholesaler's name and address in cobalt blue script: "Cushman & Co., Importers of Wines and Brandies, 376 and 378 Broadway, Albany, NY." Minor chips. (ARTHUR AUCTIONEERING)
Very Good Quality/Excellent Condition *$175 (A)*

Three gallon Evan R. Jones Pittston, PA
Cylinder-shaped with round shoulders and strap handle. Impressed with potter's imprint. Design in cobalt blue includes initials "C.R." within diamond and "Wilkes Barre" in script. Minor rim chip. (MARLIN G. DENLINGER AUCTION)
Very Good Quality/Excellent Condition *$110 (A)*

Three gallon W. Roberts Binghamton, NY
Impressed with the potter's mark below the numeral "3." Features cobalt blue drawing of two blocky buildings with simple doors, windows, and chimneys. Single strap handle at neck. Some handle cracks. (COLLECTION OF WILLARD E. GRANDE)
Superior Quality/Excellent Condition *$5,000 (D)*

Three gallon Hamilton & Jones Greensboro, PA
Slightly bulbous with strap handle. Stenciled with potter's name and large numeral "3." Both stenciled and free-hand decoration. (ARTHUR AUCTIONEERING)
Excellent Quality/Excellent Condition *$325 (A)*

Three gallon J. Hart Sherburne, NY
Cylinder-shaped with rounded shoulders and strap handle. Impressed with potter's imprint. Incised design adorned with cobalt blue features a song bird perched atop tree branch. Large cobalt blue "3" below the design. Noticeable cracks. Some chipping. (COLLECTION OF WILLARD E. GRANDE)
Excellent Quality/Good Condition *$1,800 (D)*

Three gallon J. & E. Norton Bennington, VT
Cylinder-shaped with sloping shoulders and strap handle. Impressed with potter's name and numeral "3" in cobalt blue. Large and vivid floral design also rendered in cobalt blue. (MARLIN G. DENLINGER AUCTION)
Excellent Quality/Excellent Condition *$450 (A)*

Three gallon White's Utica, NY
Cylinder-shaped with sloping shoulders and strap handle. Impressed with potter's imprint. Small bird on flowered branch rendered in cobalt blue. (MARLIN G. DENLINGER AUCTION)
Excellent Quality/Excellent Condition *$185 (A)*

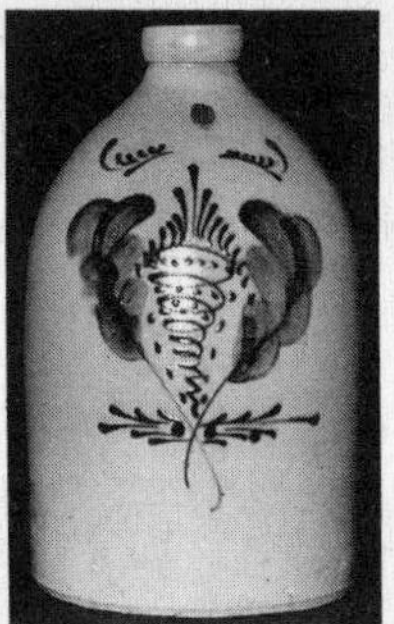

Three gallon (Maker unknown)
Cylinder-shaped with rounded shoulders and strap handle. From the Worcester, Massachusetts, pottery of Frank Norton. Skillfully decorated in cobalt blue with squiggles and leaves. (COLLECTION OF BRAD MAXWELL)
Excellent Quality/Excellent Condition *$500–$600 (D)*

Three gallon (Maker unknown)
Cylinder-shaped with rounded shoulders and strap handle. Design in cobalt blue features very plump bird perched on small branch. (MARLIN G. DENLINGER AUCTION)
Excellent Quality/Excellent Condition *$425 (A)*

Three gallon White's Utica, NY
Cylinder-shaped with rounded shoulders and strap handle. Impressed with maker's mark and numeral "3." First-class floral design rendered in cobalt blue. Damaged handle. (COLLECTION OF WILLARD E. GRANDE)
Excellent Quality/Excellent Condition *$1,000 (D)*

Three gallon F. B. Norton & Co. Worcester, MA
Slightly squatty in form with strap handle. Impressed with potter's imprint and numeral "3." Very large and vivid design in cobalt blue features parrot on leafy branch. Classic. (MARLIN G. DENLINGER AUCTION)
Excellent Quality/Excellent Condition *$1,000 (A)*

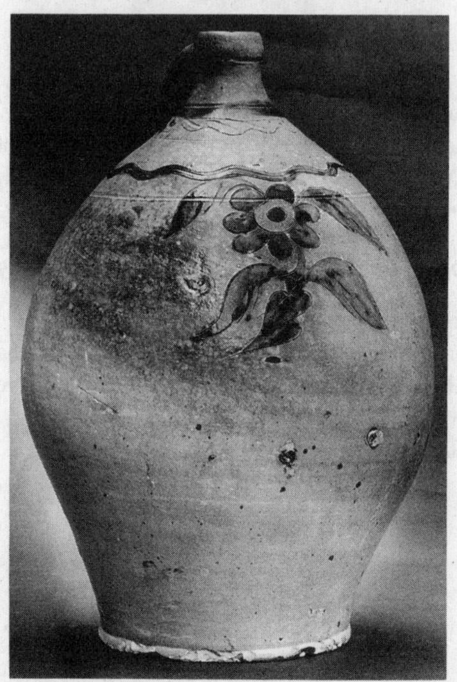

Three gallon (Maker unknown)
Ovoid in form with strap handle. Incised floral design decorated in cobalt blue. Coggled and banded near top. Produced from 1790 to 1810. Many base chips. (COLLECTION OF BETTY AND JOEL SCHATZBERG)
Excellent Quality/Good Condition *$2,000–$2,500 (D)*

Three gallon Lehman & Riedinger Poughkeepsie, NY
Ovoid in form with strap handle. Impressed with potter's imprint. Double-flower design rendered in cobalt blue. (MARLIN G. DENLINGER AUCTION)
Excellent Quality/Excellent Condition *$360 (A)*

Three gallon (Maker unknown)
Cylinder-shaped with sloping shoulders. Single strap handle. Impressed with owner's name: HART BROTHERS & CO., DEALERS IN GROCERIES AND PROVISIONS, and numeral "3." DEALERS IN impressed a second time. Bears striking cobalt blue floral design. (COLLECTION OF BRAD MAXWELL)
Excellent Quality/Excellent Condition *$450–$700 (D)*

Three gallon J. S. Taft & Co. Keene, NH
Cylinder-shaped with rounded shoulders and strap handle. Impressed with potter's imprint. Decorated in cobalt blue with triple-leaf design. (MARLIN G. DENLINGER AUCTION)
Excellent Quality/Excellent Condition *$175 (A)*

Three gallon S. Hart Fulton, NY
Ovoid in shape with heavy strap handle. Impressed with potter's imprint. Blazoned with large "3" and squiggles in cobalt blue. Minor chip. (MARLIN G. DENLINGER AUCTION)
Excellent Quality/Excellent Condition *$175 (A)*

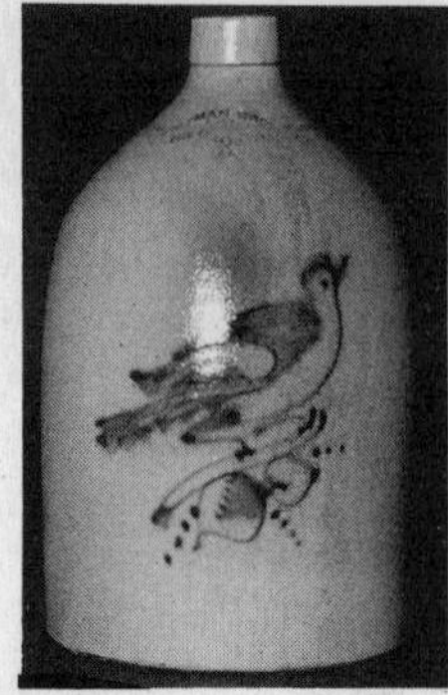

Three gallon Ottman Brothers Fort Edward, NY
Rounded shoulders, strap handle. Impressed with potter's mark and numeral "3." Conventional bird design in cobalt blue. (COLLECTION OF BRAD MAXWELL)
Good Quality/Excellent Condition *$650–$750 (D)*

Three gallon (Maker unknown)
Cylinder-shaped with rounded shoulders and strap handle. Decorated with cobalt blue rendering of a basket filled with flowers. Rim chip. (MARLIN G. DENLINGER AUCTION)
Excellent Quality/Excellent Condition *$150 (A)*

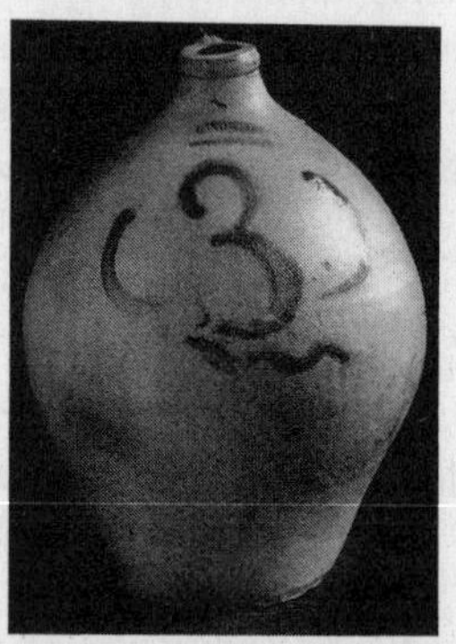

Three gallon L. Norton Bennington, VT
Ovoid in form. Impressed with potter's mark. Decorated in front with giant "3" in cobalt blue and big squiggles beneath and at the sides. Kiln damage at front and back. (COLLECTION OF WILLARD E. GRANDE)
Excellent Quality/Very Good Condition *$600 (D)*

Three gallon W. Roberts Binghamton, NY
Cylinder-shaped with sloping shoulders. Impressed with potter's imprint. Simple floral design rendered in cobalt blue. (MARLIN G. DENLINGER AUCTION)
Excellent Quality/Excellent Condition *$150 (A)*

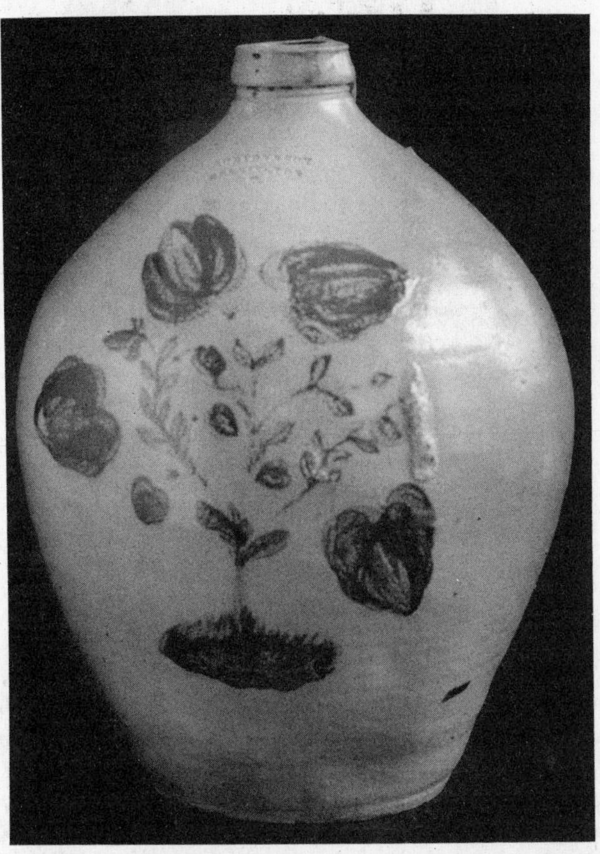

Three gallon L. Norton & Sons Bennington, VT
Ovoid in shape with strap handle. Impressed with potter's imprint. Design in brown ocher, not cobalt blue, depicts stalks from a rose-bush or similar plant. Dates to the 1830s. Some kiln damage. (COLLECTION OF WILLARD E. GRANDE)
Excellent Quality/Very Good Condition *$3,800 (D)*

Four gallon (Maker unknown)
Ovoid in form with strap handle. Simple floral design and numeral "4" rendered in cobalt blue. (MARLIN G. DENLINGER AUCTION)
Excellent Quality/Excellent Condition *$175 (A)*

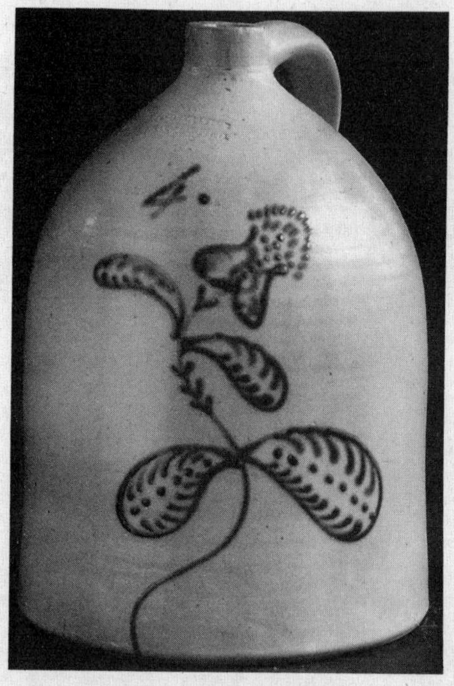

Four gallon Lyons Co-operative Pottery Co. Lyons, NY
Cylinder-shaped with sloping shoulders and heavy strap handle. Impressed with potter's imprint. Simple floral design in cobalt blue. Dates to first decade of twentieth century. (COLLECTION OF WILLARD E. GRANDE)
Excellent Quality/Excellent Condition *$400 (D)*

Four gallon E. A. Montell Olean, NY
Slightly squatty with sloping shoulders and strap handle. Impressed with potter's imprint and numeral "4." Very large, vivid, and attractive cluster of flowers rendered in cobalt blue. Hairline crack. (MARLIN G. DENLINGER AUCTION)
Excellent Quality/Excellent Condition *$475 (A)*

Four gallon Fulper Brothers Flemington, NJ
Cylinder-shaped with sloping shoulders and strap handle. Impressed with maker's mark and large numeral "4." Skillfully decorated in cobalt blue with pair of performing acrobats—a man garbed in checked trousers and dark jacket and holding a top hat standing erect, and a woman performing a handstand, her feet at the man's neck. Extremely rare. Piece fetched the price listed below at Sotheby's auction in 1986. (COLLECTION OF BETTY AND JOEL SCHATZBERG)

Superior Quality/Excellent Condition *$28,600 (A)*

Four gallon Lyons Co-operative Pottery Co. Lyons, NY
Cylinder-shaped with sloping shoulders and strap handle. Impressed with potter's name. Large design features four-leaved thistle plant rendered in cobalt blue; also, numeral "4." (MARLIN G. DENLINGER AUCTION)
Excellent Quality/Excellent Condition *$225 (A)*

Five gallon New York Stoneware Co. Fort Edward, NY
Cylinder-shaped with sloping shoulders and strap handle. Impressed with potter's imprint. "John O'Neil, Whitehall" blazoned across front in cobalt blue script. Hairline crack. (MARLIN G. DENLINGER AUCTION)
Excellent Quality/Excellent Condition *$200 (A)*

Five gallon (Maker unknown)
Cylinder-shaped with sloping shoulders and pair of strap handles. Impressed with numeral "5" and user's name: GEORGE HAYT, LIQUOR DEALER, SENECA FALLS. Decorated in cobalt blue with plump, long-billed bird perched on a leafy branch. Pencil-size puncture at front. (COLLECTION OF WILLARD E. GRANDE)
Good Quality/Good Condition *$950 (D)*

Five gallon A. K. Ballard Bennington, VT
Straight-sided with rounded shoulders. Impressed with maker's name and numeral "5." Cobalt blue decoration depicts a spray of grapes and handful of leaves. (COLLECTION OF WILLARD E. GRANDE)
Excellent Quality/Good Condition *$850 (D)*

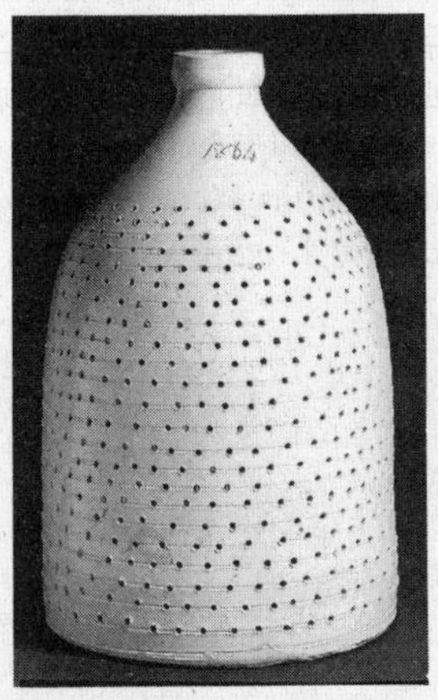

(Capacity unknown) (Maker unknown)
Cylinder-shaped with sloping shoulders. No handle. Highly unusual piece that features many hundreds of pencil-size holes arranged in twenty-three parallel rows. Believed to be used for filtering water or perhaps as a leech storage vessel. The date "1864" is incised near top. (LITCHFIELD AUCTION GALLERY)
Excellent Quality/Excellent Condition *$675 (A)*

(Capacity unknown) (Maker unknown)
Ovoid in form with threaded neck. Incised design decorated in cobalt blue depicts a raven-type bird perched on a leafy branch. Piece dates to mid-nineteenth century. (LITCHFIELD AUCTION GALLERY)
Excellent Quality/Excellent Condition *$2,800 (A)*

Mugs

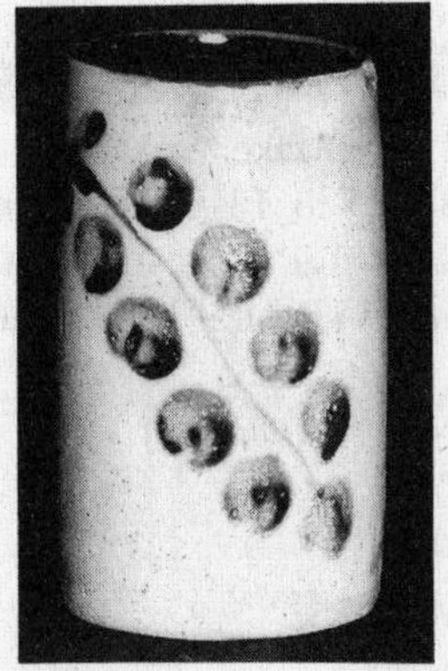

One pint (Maker unknown)
Double row of eight cobalt blue grapes extend diagonally from top to bottom, divided by a diagonal line with a grape at each end. Dates to 1830s. Small rim chips. One of a kind. (COLLECTION OF BRAD MAXWELL)
Excellent Quality/Good Condition *$1,800–$2,000 (D)*

(Capacity unknown) (Maker unknown)
Barrel-shaped with strap handle. Pair of blue bands and coggle wheel decoration at top and bottom. (ARTHUR AUCTIONEERING)
Excellent Quality/Excellent Condition *$70 (A)*

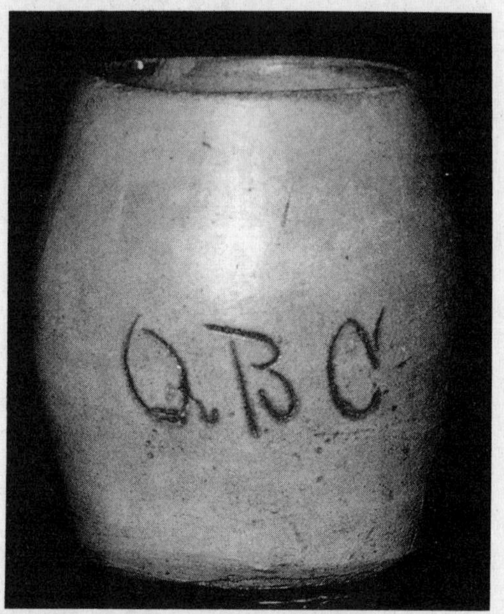

(Capacity unknown) (Maker unknown)
Unusual keg shape. Dates to 1810. Bears initials Q.B.C. in cobalt blue, believed to stand for Quinsigamond Boat Club. (Lake Quinsigamond is located in central Massachusetts.) (COLLECTION OF BRAD MAXWELL)
Excellent Quality/Excellent Condition *$475–$500 (D)*

Pitchers

One quart (Maker unknown)
Very wide mouth with long strap handle that extends from top to base. Decorated with free-hand drawing of long-billed bird in cobalt blue. Attributed to Fulper Brothers, Flemington, New Jersey, potters. Some rim chips. Unique. (COLLECTION OF WILLARD E. GRANDE)
Excellent Quality/Excellent Condition *$1,900 (D)*

Two quart (Maker unknown)
Ovoid in shape with strap handle. Double-banded in cobalt blue at neck. Bold cobalt blue decoration at front and back. (ARTHUR AUCTIONEERING)
Excellent Quality/Excellent Condition *$425 (A)*

One gallon (Maker unknown)
Baluster-shaped with strap handle. Attributed to Sipe, Nichols & Co., Williamsport, Pennsylvania, potters. Floral decoration in cobalt blue. Blue at handle. Minor rim chips. (ARTHUR AUCTIONEERING)
Very Good Quality/Excellent Condition *$350 (A)*

One gallon James Hamilton & Co. Greensboro, PA
Baluster-shaped with strap handle. Potter's name stenciled at bottom. Stenciled and free-hand decoration. Spout chip; crack at side. (ARTHUR AUCTIONEERING)
Excellent Quality/Good Condition *$250 (A)*

One gallon White's Binghamton, NY
Baluster-shaped with strap handle. Impressed with potter's imprint. Design in cobalt blue features poppylike flower. Minor rim chip. (MARLIN G. DENLINGER AUCTION)
Excellent Quality/Excellent Condition *$325 (A)*

One gallon (Maker unknown)
Baluster-shaped with strap handle. Simple floral design rendered in cobalt blue. Minor rim chip. (MARLIN G. DENLINGER AUCTION)
Excellent Quality/Excellent Condition *$180 (A)*

One gallon (Maker unknown)
Baluster-shaped with strap handle. Both interior and exterior glazed in Albany slip. (ARTHUR AUCTIONEERING)
Good Quality/Excellent Condition *$85 (A)*

Two gallon John Schmidt Rochester, NY
Baluster-shaped with strap handle. Impressed with maker's imprint. Floral design in cobalt blue decorated with small polka dots. Blue at handle. Hairline crack. (ARTHUR AUCTIONEERING)
Excellent Quality/Excellent Condition *$425 (A)*

Two gallon M. C. Webster & Son Hartford, CT
Baluster-shaped with strap handle. Impressed with potter's imprint over which light cobalt blue has been brushed. (MARLIN G. DENLINGER AUCTION)
Excellent Quality/Excellent Condition *$150 (A)*

Two gallon (Maker unknown)
Baluster-shaped with strap handle. Floral design in cobalt blue. Professionally restored. (ARTHUR AUCTIONEERING)
Excellent Quality/Good Condition *$375 (A)*

Three gallon (Maker unknown)
Boston-style brown-glaze pitcher, attributed to Jonathan Fenton. Heavy strap handle. Chipped snout. (COLLECTION OF ED FARIA)
Excellent Quality/Excellent Condition *$450 (D)*

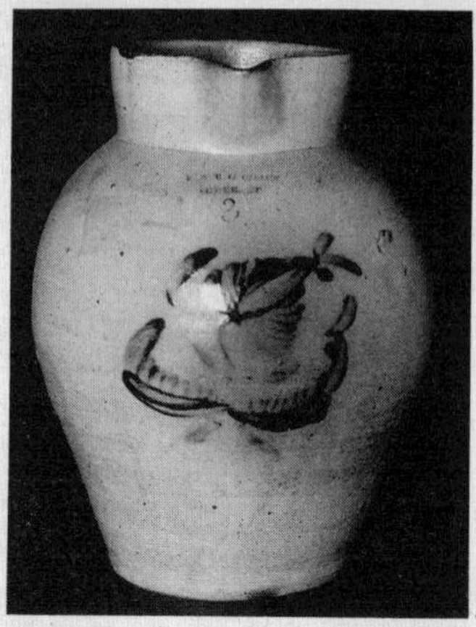

Three gallon L. & B. G. Chace Somerset, MA
Bulbous body and heavy strap handle. Impressed with maker's name and numeral "3." Floral design at front. Unusual for its size. (COLLECTION OF BRAD MAXWELL)
Excellent Quality/Excellent Condition *$1,500–$2,000 (D)*

(Capacity unknown) (Maker unknown)
Baluster-shaped. Large and handsome cobalt blue floral decoration at front. Believed to have been produced by the New Jersey pottery of Jakob Wingender & Sons during the mid-nineteenth century. (LITCHFIELD AUCTION GALLERY)
Very Good Quality/Excellent Condition *$375 (A)*

Spittoons

(Capacity unknown) (Maker unknown)
Squat cylinder with closed lip angling downward to large opening in center. Circular opening in side to facilitate cleaning. Coated with Albany slip at top and within. Small decoration in cobalt blue. Attributed to White's Pottery, Utica, New York. Minor chipping. (COLLECTION OF WILLARD E. GRANDE)
Excellent Quality/Excellent Condition *$200 (D)*

(Capacity unknown) (Maker unknown)
Brown-glazed with concave sides. Top angled downward to hole in center. Circular opening at side to aid in cleaning. Brushed all around with cobalt blue. (ARTHUR AUCTIONEERING)
Very Good Quality/Excellent Condition *$100 (A)*

Water Coolers

Two gallon W. A. Lewis Galesville, NY

Impressed with the potter's mark. Features striking cobalt blue basket-of-flowers decoration. Opening for spigot at piece's base is incorporated into the artwork. Minor rim chip. Impressive. (COLLECTION OF WILLARD E. GRANDE)

Superior Quality/Good Condition *$5,000 (D)*

Two gallon T. Seymour Troy, NY
Classically ovoid in form with pair of strap handles at neck. Impressed with potter's mark. Small floral design in cobalt blue. Hole for spigot at base. Minor chips. (LITCHFIELD AUCTION GALLERY)
Superior Quality/Excellent Condition *$6,000 (A)*

Three gallon (Maker unknown)
Barrel-shaped with opening in base for spigot. Decorated with four horizontal bands in cobalt blue. (MARLIN G. DENLINGER AUCTION)
Excellent Quality/Excellent Condition *$130 (A)*

Four gallon O. L. & A. K. Ballard Burlington, VT
Barrel-shaped with opening in base for spigot. Impressed with potter's imprint. Decorated with eight horizontal bands and very bold floral design rendered in cobalt blue. Hairline crack. (MARLIN G. DENLINGER AUCTION)
Excellent Quality/Excellent Condition *$350 (A)*

Four gallon (Maker unknown)
Ovoid in shape with opening in base for spigot. Embossed, applied decoration featuring pair of eagles and the phrase *e pluribus unum* ("out of many, one," motto of the United States). Cobalt blue dabbed around spigot opening and handles. Double-banded near top. Crack at back. (MARLIN G. DENLINGER AUCTION)
Excellent Quality/Very Good Condition *$175 (A)*

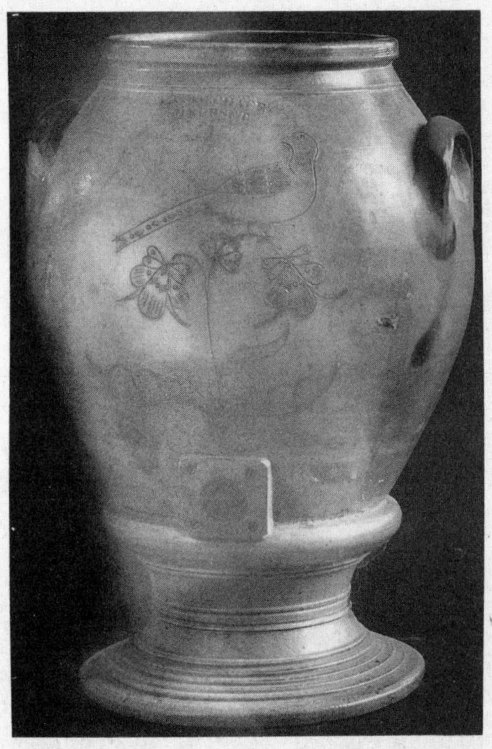

Four gallon L. & B. G. Chace Somerset, MA
Ovoid in shape on a turned base. Impressed with potter's mark. Lug handles. Opening for spigot at base. Features the incised design of a bird perched atop a flowering plant on the front and a cobalt blue flower on the back. Some hairline cracks and flaking. Very rare. (COLLECTION OF WILLARD E. GRANDE)
Superior Quality/Good Condition *$3,500 (D)*

Five gallon (approx.) (Maker unknown)
Vase-shaped vessel with hole for spigot at bottom and separate base. Features incised folksy design of small running horse outlined in cobalt blue. Unusual. Crack at back. (MARLIN G. DENLINGER AUCTION)
Excellent Quality/Good Condition *$400 (A)*

Six gallon Charlestown pottery MA
Barrel-shaped with spigot at base. CHARLESTOWN and numeral "8" impressed near top. Colorfully decorated with floral sprigs in cobalt blue and with pairs of blue horizontal bands that encircle the piece and which are meant to represent the metal banding on a wooden barrel. Outstanding. (COLLECTION OF BETTY AND JOEL SCHATZBERG)
Superior Quality/Excellent Condition *$10,000–$13,000 (D)*

Resources

Museums and Historical Societies

Museums or historical societies in areas of the country that once produced stoneware are usually excellent sources of background information. These institutions frequently own outstanding collections, portions of which are on exhibit. The Bennington Museum (West Main St., Bennington, Vermont 05201) displays the country's largest collection of Bennington ware, along with exhibits of potters' tools and equipment. The Bucks County Historical Society (Pine St., Doylestown, Pennsylvania 18901) offers an exceptional collection of Pennsylvania stoneware. The New York Historical Society (170 Central Park West, New York, New York 10023) owns and exhibits spectacular examples of the output of early New York potters. The Henry Ford Museum and Greenfield Village (20900 Oakwood Blvd., Dearborn, Michigan 48121) boasts an excellent stoneware collection that is on permanent display.

An impressive private collection, owned by Willard E. Grande, is on exhibit at the Regent Street Antique Center in Saratoga Springs, New York (153 Regent St., Saratoga Springs, New York 12866).

Books and Other Publications

The illustrated catalogs issued by auction houses in connection with their stoneware sales are an excellent guide to market conditions. Particularly recommended are those published by Marlin Denlinger (RR 3, Box 3775, Morrisville, Vermont 05661) in connection with his stoneware auctions held each April and October. Each catalog is $12 up to the time of the sale, and $10 after the sale. The post-sale catalog includes a price list.

Most of the better known antiques magazines are not of great value when it comes to stoneware because they are not consistent in their coverage of the field. More worthwhile are each of several regional publications, particularly *Antiques and the Arts Weekly* (Bee Publishing Co., Inc., 5 Church Hill Rd., Newtown, Connecticut, $35 a year). Known colloquially as the "Newtown Bee," it's a hefty newspaper that reports knowledgeably on the New England stoneware scene. *Maine*

Antique Digest (71 Main St., Waldoboro, Maine 04572, monthly, $29 per year), and *The New York-Pennsylvania Collector* (Wolfe Publications, Inc., Drawer C, Fishers, New York, monthly, $15 per year) provide coverage of their respective regions.

There are scores of books that can be helpful too. Check your local library. At many antique and collectible shows, at least one dealer is on hand who offers books on collecting specialities. One example is The Reference Rack, Box 445C, Orefield, Pennsylvania 18069. Write for a catalog of titles available. It costs $1. While such dealers specialize in recently published volumes, they are willing to order a specific title as long as it is in print.

You may also want to check one or more of the following worthwhile books on stoneware:

Barret, Richard Carter: *Bennington Pottery and Porcelain.* New York: Bonanza Books, 1958.

A discussion of not merely conventional stoneware, but also other examples of decorative ware produced by the potters of Bennington. Amply illustrated.

Brainin, M. Lelyn: *The Early Makers of Handcrafted Earthenware and Stoneware in Central and Southern New Jersey*. Rutherford, New Jersey: Fairleigh Dickinson University Press, 1988.

An in-depth study, along with an excellent checklist.

Brainin, M. Lelyn: *The Early Potters and Potteries of Maine*. Middletown, Connecticut: Wesleyan University Press, 1978.

A detailed study of Maine's stoneware and earthenware potters. Excellent checklist.

Greer, Georgeanna H.: *American Stonewares; The Art and Craft of Utilitarian Potters*. Exton, Pennsylvania: Schiffer Publishing, Ltd., 1981.

Written by a respected author and long-time collector, this is a comprehensive and authoritative study of stoneware history and the technology of production.

Contains excellent chapters on glaze, potter's marks and decorations, and regional stoneware variations. More than 350 photographs. A highly recommended reference.

Guilland, Harold F.: *Early American Folk Pottery*. Philadelphia, Pennsylvania: Chilton Book Co., 1971.

A well-done introduction to the field.

Horne, Catherine Wilson (Editor): *Crossroads of Clay; The Southern Alkaline-Glazed Stoneware Tradition*. Columbia, South Carolina: McKissick Museum, University of South Carolina, 1990.

A collection of four authoritative essays dealing with the ceramic tradition that developed in South Carolina and spread into Georgia, North Carolina, Alabama, Mississippi, and Texas. Interesting and informative. Excellent photographs.

Ketchum, William C., Jr.: *Early Potters and Potteries of New York State, 1650–1900*. Second Edition. Syracuse, New York: Syracuse University Press, 1987.

A detailed study of New York potters with a reliable and comprehensive checklist. Recommended.

Ketchum, William C., Jr.: *American Stoneware*. New York: Henry Holt, 1991.

Leder, Steven B., and Cesana, Fred: *The Birds of Bennington*. Hamden, Connecticut: Stoneware Publications, 1992.

A serious study of a popular specialty, with more than forty-five color photos and a "rarity guide."

Osgood, Cornelias: *The Jug and Related Stoneware of Bennington*. Rutland, Vermont: Charles E. Tuttle Co., 1971.

A comprehensive study of the stoneware produced at the Norton potteries in Bennington, Vermont.

Ramsey, John: *American Potters and Pottery*. Clinton, Massachusetts: Hale, Cushman, and Flint, 1929.

A standard reference for background information on American potteries, with a section on potter's marks and a pottery checklist.

Spargo, John: *Early American Pottery and China*. Rutland, Vermont: Charles E. Tuttle Co., 1974.

A study of the manufacture of stoneware, earthenware, and American china in the Northeast and Atlantic states. First published in 1926. Limited number of illustrations.

Steward, Regina, and Cosentino, Geraldine: *Stoneware; A Guide for Beginners*. New York: Golden Press, 1977.

An attractive, easy-to-read introduction to collecting stoneware.

Watkins, Laura Woodside: *Early New England Potters and Their Wares*. Cambridge, Massachusetts: Harvard University Press, 1950.

Perhaps the best source for general information on New England stoneware. Also discusses earthenware. Excellent checklist.

Watkins, Laura Woodside: *Early New England Pottery*. Sturbridge, Massachusetts: Old Sturbridge Village, 1966.

A short book discussing the work of early New England potters.

Webster, Donald Blake: *Decorated Stoneware and Pottery of North America*. Rutland, Vermont: Charles E. Tuttle Co., 1980.

A well-researched and amply illustrated discussion of American stoneware. Good chapters on specialties: flowers, birds, human figures, etc.; also a pottery checklist. Recommended.

Potters and Potteries

The following list is meant to help in establishing the approximate age of marked pieces of stoneware. It was compiled from many sources, including business directories, the publications of museums and historical societies, and other books.

It is not a complete list, since many of the stoneware potteries that once operated are not known today. In addition, for more than a few potteries that are known to have existed, the dates of operation have never been reliably established. In the nation's earliest days, the opening of a stoneware pottery was not a matter usually thought to be worth officially noting. Records of towns in which potteries are known to have operated often contain no mention of them. Official town records generally note the founding of a gristmill, a sawmill, even a distillery, but the town pottery receives no mention. To determine the names of potteries, it has often been necessary to examine the descriptive clauses of deeds of title.

Contributing to the problem is the fact that individual potteries sometimes produced their crocks, jugs, and other wares almost in anonymity. During the early decades of the nineteenth century, Americans often turned their backs on American products in favor of those made in Europe. It wasn't that American-made products were not the equal of imported goods in terms of workmanship; it had simply become chic to buy from abroad. So it was that American pottery makers of the early decades of the nineteenth century often left their wares unmarked. The name or logo of an American potter in a jug or jar could be a reason for rejection. The United States Pottery at Bennington, Vermont, for example, often received orders from retailers that their goods not be marked. They then could be sold as English wares to American customers who scorned American products.

More is known about early potteries in New York, New Jersey, much of Pennsylvania, and New England than elsewhere. Less is known about potteries in the mid-Atlantic states and the Midwest. As studies applying to these areas are completed, this list will be amended.

Abbe, Frederick
Columbus, OH, c. 1848–50

Adams, Allison & Co.
Middlebury, OH, c. 1860

Addington, S.
Utica, NY, c. 1830–38

Adley & Co.
Ithaca, NY, c. 1860–80

Allison, W. B. & Co.
Middlebury, OH, c. 1865–75

Amos, William
Baltimore, MD, 1833–37

Armstrong & Wentworth
Norwich, CT, 1814–34

Atcheson, H. S.
Annapolis, IN, c. 1841–1906

Athens Pottery
Athens, NY, 1893–1900

Atwater, Caleb & Joseph
Atwater, OH, c. 1830–40

Bagnall, George
Newcomerstown, OH, c. 1870–75

Bakewell, H. N.
Wellsburg, WV, c. 1831–41

Baldosen & Pace
Roseville, OH, 1875

Ballard, A. K.
Burlington, VT, c. 1867–72

Ballard, O. L. & A. K.
Burlington, VT, 1856–72

Bangor Stoneware
Bangor, ME, c. 1890–1916

Beckting Brothers
Evansville, IN, 1885–1900

Beckting Brothers
Huntingburg, IN, c. 1870–1900

Beecher & Lantz
Akron, OH, 1863–

Bell, John
Waynesboro, PA, 1833–81

Bell, Joseph
Putnam, OH, 1827–50

Bell, M. C.
Cornwall, NY, c. 1830–50

Bell, S.
Strasburg, VA, 1833–53

Bell, S. & S.
Strasburg, VA, 1853–82

Bell & Sons
Strasburg, VA, 1882–1908

Bell, Upton
Waynesboro, PA, 1895–99

Bendenbohl, Peter
Akron, OH, 1863–

Bennett & Chollar
Homer, NY, 1837–39

Bennett, E. & W.
Baltimore, MD, c. 1849–56

Bennett, Edwin
Baltimore, MD, 1846–49

Binkley, George
Canton, OH, c. 1826–40

Bissett Pottery
Old Bridge, NJ, 1800–50

Blair, Sylvester
Cortland, NY, 1829–35

Bodenbuhl, Peter
Akron, OH, c. 1863–70

Bodine, J.
Putnam, OH, c. 1836–45

Boerner, Shapley & Vogt
Massilon Stoneware Co.
Massilon, OH, 1882–1900

Bonnin, Gousse & Morris, George Anthony
Philadelphia, PA, 1769–

Boone, Benjamin
Brooklyn, NY, 1846–63

Boone, T. G. & Sons
Brooklyn, NY 1842–46

Boone, Thomas E.
Brooklyn, NY, 1858–64

Booth Brothers
East Liverpool, OH, 1858–65

Boston Pottery Co.
Boston, MA, 1878–c. 1900

Bowne, Catherine
Cheesequake, NJ, 1815–39

Boynton, C.
Albany, NY, 1818–24
Troy, NY, 1829–36

Boynton & Co.
Troy, NY, 1826–29

Boynton, J.
Albany, NY, 1816–18

Brady & Ryan
Ellenville, NY, c. 1887–c. 1902

Braun, C. W.
Buffalo, NY, 1856–96

Brayton, J. F.
Utica, NY, 1833–c. 1837

Brayton, Kellogg & Doolittle
Utica, NY, 1827–c. 1840

Brewer & Halm
Havana, NY, 1853–54

Brewer, S. T.
Havana, NY, 1854–60

Bricker, John
Albany, NY, 1842–48

Bromley & Son
Cincinnati, OH, 1860–c. 1870

Bromley, William
Cincinnati, OH, 1843–60

Broome & Morgan
Dayton, OH, 1882–c. 1900

Brown Brothers
Huntington, NY, 1863–80

Brown & McKenzie
East River, WV, c. 1870–1900

Bullard, J. O. & Scott, A. F.
Allston, MA, c. 1870–1909

Bullock, W.
Roseville, OH, c. 1870–75

Burchfield, Adam
Pittsburgh, PA, 1860–65

Burger, J., Jr.
Rochester, NY, 1878–90

Burger, John
Rochester, NY, 1854–67

Burgess, Webster & Viney
East Liverpool, OH, 1867–69

Burley, John
Mount Sterling, OH, c. 1840–50

Burney, J. M.
Jordan, NY, c. 1850–60

Burns, W. F.
Atwater, OH, 1850–74

Butler, & Co., A. J.
New Brunswick, NJ, c. 1850–67

Caire, Adam
Poughkeepsie, NY, 1878–96

Caire & Co., John B.
Poughkeepsie, NY, 1845–52

Caire, Frederick J.
Huntington, NY, 1854–63

Caire, Jacob
Poughkeepsie, NY, 1845–48

Caire Pottery, Jacob
Poughkeepsie, NY, 1852–54

Camp, Cook & Co.
Cuyahoga Falls, OH, 1863–c. 1880

Campbell, Justin
Utica, NY, 1826–c. 1840

Carlyle & McFadden
Freeman's Landing, WV, 1850–53

Carpenter, Frederick (Edmands Pottery)
Charlestown, MA, 1812–27

Central New York Pottery
Utica, NY, 1877–82

Chapman, Josiah
Troy, NY, c. 1815–c. 1819

Chollar & Bennett
Cortland, NY, 1842–44

Chollar & Darby
Cortland, NY, 1844–49

Chollar & Darby
Homer, NY, 1839–44

Chollar, Thomas
Cortland, NY, 1832–42

Clark & Co.
Lyons, NY, 1822–52

Clark & Co., J.
Troy, NY, c. 1826–27

Clark & Co., Nathan
Lyons, NY, 1822–52

Clark & Co., Nathan
Mount Morris, 1835–46

Clark & Fox
Athens, NY, 1829–38

Clark, Nathan
Athens, NY, 1813–29

Clark, Nathan
Rochester, NY, c. 1841–52

Clark, Nathan, Jr.
Athens, NY, 1843–91

Clough, Calhoun & Co.
Portland, ME, 1847–48

Cole Pottery
Seagrove, NC, 1891–19

Columbian Pottery
Perth Amboy, NJ, c. 1830–35

Commeraw, Thomas
New York, NY, 1795–97, 1802–c. 1820

Congress Pottery
South Amboy, NJ, 1828–c. 1853

Cook & Co., Fairbanks
Akron, OH, c. 1880–87

Cook & Richardson
Akron, OH, 1870

Cowden, F. H.
Harrisburg, PA, 1881–88

Cowden, J. W.
Harrisburg, PA, c. 1861–70

Cowden & Son, F. H.
Harrisburg, PA, 1888–1904

Cowden & Wilcox
Harrisburg, PA, c. 1870–90

Coxe, Daniell
Burlington, NJ, 1634–

Crafts & Co., Caleb
Whately, MA, 1845–54

Crafts & Co., Caleb
Portland, ME, c. 1835–41

Crafts Family
Whately, MA, 1806–61

Crafts, Martin
Nashua, NH, 1838–52

Crafts, Martin
Whately, MA, 1857–61

Crolius, Clarkson
New York, NY, 1790–

Crolius, Clarkson, Jr.
New York, NY, c. 1835–48

Crolius, John William
New York, NY, c. 1728–c. 1775

Crolius, William
New York, NY, c. 1770–c. 1779

Crolius, William & Crolius, Peter
New York, NY, 1737–

Cross, Peter
Hartford, CT, 1805–18

Cushman, Paul
Albany, NY, 1807–33

Darrow, John
Baldwinsville, NY, 1860–74

Darrow & Sons
Baldwinsville, NY, c. 1855–c. 1872

Dick, Jacob
Tuscarawas County, Ohio, c. 1830–40

Dillon, Charles
Albany, NY, c. 1825–42

Dillon, Henry
Albany, NY, 1835–39

Dillon & Porter
Albany, NY, 1840–42

Donahue Pottery
Parkersburg, WV, 1866–1908

Dorchester Pottery Works
Dorchester, MA, c. 1880

Durell, Jonathan
New York, NY, 1753–74

Eagle Pottery Co.
Macomb, IL, c. 1883–1900

Eaton, Jacob & Stout, Samuel
Washington, NJ, 1818–45

Edmands, Barnabas & Burroughs, William
Charlestown, MA, 1812–50

Edmands & Co.
Boston, MA, 1812–1905

Edmands & Hooper
Charlestown, MA, c. 1868–1905

Eichenlaub, Valentine
Cincinnati, OH, c. 1852–

Eichert, Peter & Fleckinger, Jacob
Orrville, OH, 1877–1900

Emsinger, A. Jonathan
Creek, OH, c. 1828–40

Enterprise Pottery Co.
Brighton, PA, c. 1880–1900

Fallston Pottery Co.
Fallston, PA, c. 1875–1900

Farrar, Ebenezer L.
Burlington, VT, c. 1850–71

Farrar, G. W. & J. H.
Fairfax, VT, c. 1840–59

Farrar, Isaac Brown
Fairfax, VT, c. 1815–38

Farrar & Stearns
Fairfax, VT, 1851–52

Farrar, W. H.
Geddes, NY, 1841–58

Farrar, W. H.
Syracuse, NY, 1858–71

Farrington & Co.
Elmira, NY, 1886–87

Farrington, E. W.
Elmira, NY, 1887–c. 1895

Fayette & Co.
Utica, NY, 1833–c. 1837

Fenton, J. H.
Mogadore, OH, c. 1854–75

Fenton, Jacob
New Haven, CT, 1790–1801

Fenton, Jonathan
Boston, MA, 1794–96
Walpole, NH, 1797–1801
Dorset, VT, 1801–c. 1840

Fenton, Richard
St. Johnsbury, VT, 1808–59

Field, T. F.
Utica, NY, 1828–30

Fish, C.
Swan Hill Pottery
South Amboy, NJ, 1849–50

Fisher, J. & Co.
Lyons, NY, 1872–c. 1882

Fisher, Jacob
Lyons, NY, c. 1882–1902

Fisher & McLain
Hillsboro, OH, c. 1810–40

Fisher, Thomas
Steubenville, OH, 1808–c. 1825

Fisk, D. & Co.
Cleveland, OH, c. 1835–37

Fort Edward Pottery Co.
Fort Edward, NY, 1859–61

Fort Edward Stoneware Co.
Fort Edward, NY, 1875–c. 1882

Fossbender, N.
Mogadore, OH, 1860–75

Fowler & McKenzie
Vanport, PA, 1870–1900

Fox, E. S.
Athens, NY, 1838–43

French, Eben
Chatfield Corners, OH, c. 1837–45

Furman, Noah
South Amboy, NJ, 1846–56

Gardiner Stone Ware Co.
Gardiner, ME, c. 1874–87

Geddes Stone Ware Pottery Co.
Geddes, NY, 1883–87

Gideon, Crisbaum & Co.
Poughkeepsie, NY, 1853–54

Glasgow Pottery Co.
Trenton, NJ. 1860–90

Goodale, Daniel, Jr., & Co.
Hartford, CT, 1818–30

Goodale & Stedman
Hartford, CT, 1822–25

Goodwin, Horace & Webster, Mack
Hartford, CT, c. 1810–40

Goodwin & Sons
Hartford, CT, 1795–1832

Gossett, Amariah
Hillsboro, OH, c. 1810–40

Graves, D. W.
Westmoreland, NY, c. 1855–c. 1875

Greble, Benjamin
Baltimore, MD, 1837–50

Green, Adam
New Brunswick, NJ, 1840–80

Greenland, N. W.
Cassville, PA, c. 1885–1900

Guy, G. S. & Co.
Fort Edward, NY, c. 1882–c. 1885

Haidle & Co.
Newark, NJ, 1871–75

Haidle & Zipf
Union Pottery
Newark, NJ, 1875–77

Hall, Amos & Cochran, Robert
Orrville, OH, c. 1862–77

Hamilton, James & Co.
Eagle Pottery
Greensboro, PA, 1844–c. 1885

Hamlyn, George
Bridgeton, NJ, c. 1835–70

Hancock, Frederick
Worcester, MA, 1858–

Hancock, John & Hancock, William
Congress Pottery
South Amboy, NJ, 1828–c. 1847

Hanford, Isaac
Hartford, CT, 1796–

Hanlen, Bernard
Trenton, NJ, c. 1775–80

Harmon, Christian
Salem, OH, c. 1825–40

Harrington & Burger
Rochester, NY, 1852–54

Harrington, Thompson
Hartford, CT, c. 1840–52
Lyons, NY, 1852–72

Harris, Thomas
Cuyahoga Falls, OH, 1863–c.

Harris, W. P.
Newtown Township, OH, c. 1828–56

Hart, Charles
Ogdensburg, NY, 1850–58
Sherburne, NY, 1841–50, 1858–c. 1885

Hart, Delos
Akron, OH, c. 1880

Hart, James
Sherburne, NY, 1841–58

Hart, James & Hart, Samuel
Oswego, NY, 1830–32
Oswego Falls, NY, 1832–41

Hart, Samuel
Oswego, NY, 1830–c. 1865
Picton, Ont., 1849–74

Hart, William
Picton, Ont., 1849–55

Hastings & Belding
S. Ashfield, MA, 1850–56

Hathaway, Charles E.
Somerset, MA, 1882–c. 1900

Havens, Samuel
Putnam, OH, c. 1836–46

Hawthorn Pottery Co.
Hawthorn, PA, 1894–c. 1928

Haxstun & Co.
Fort Edward, NY, 1857–c. 1900

Haxstun, Ottman & Co.
Fort Edward, NY, 1867–72

Heighshoe, S. E.
Somerset, OH, c. 1850

Heiser, J.
Buffalo, NY, 1852–56

Henderson, D. & Henderson, J.
Jersey City, NJ, 1828–45

Henry, Jacob
Albany, NY, 1827–34

Hewell Pottery
Gillsville, GA, c. 1830–1900

Hewett, Isaac
Excelsior Works
Price's Landing, PA, c. 1870–80

Higgins, A. D.
Cleveland, OH, c. 1837–50

Hill, Foster & Co.
Akron, OH, c. 1849–51

Hill, Merrill & Co.
Akron, OH, 1851–

Hill, Powers & Co.
Akron, OH, c. 1859–68

Hilton Pottery Co.
Hickory, NC, c. 1890–1900

Hirn, Joseph & Co.
St. Louis, MO, c. 1860–69

Holmes & Purdee
Dundee, NY, c. 1845–52

Holmes & Savage
Dundee, NY, 1852–c. 1862

Houghton, Curtis & Co.
Dalton, OH, c. 1842–c. 1864

Houghton, Edwin
Dalton, OH, c. 1864–c. 1890

Houghton, Eugene
Dalton, OH, c. 1890–c. 1900

Howe & Clark
Athens, NY, 1805–13

Hubbell & Chesebro
Geddes, NY, c. 1867–84

Hudson & French
Galway, NY, c. 1860

Hudson, Nathanial
Galway, NY, c. 1850–c. 1868

Hughes, Thomas
Salem, OH, c. 1812–c. 1815

Humiston & Cummings
South Amboy, NJ, c. 1830–50

Humiston & Warner
South Amboy, NJ, c. 1830–50

Hyssong, C. B.
Cassville, PA, c. 1870–1900

Illiff, Richard
Hillsboro, OH, 1806–c. 1820

Ingell, Jonathan
West Taunton, MA, c. 1830–50

Jenkins, A.
Columbus, OH, c. 1840–50

Jennings, Andrew
Galena, IL, c. 1880–87

Johnson & Baldwin
Akron, OH, 1860

Johnson & Dewey
Akron, OH, 1860–c. 1875

Johnson, John
Staten Island, NY, c. 1793

Johnson, Whitmore & Co.
Akron, OH, 1857–60

Judd, Norman L.
Rome, NY, c. 1800–20

Kendall, L.
Chelsea, MA, 1836–c. 1870

Kendall & Sons
Cincinnati, OH, 1846–50

Kendall, Uriah
Cincinnati, OH, 1834–c. 1846

Kier, S. M.
Pittsburgh, PA, c. 1867–1900

Kirkpatrick, C. & W.
Anna Pottery Co.
Anna, IL, 1859–c. 1890

Knapp, F. K.
Akron, OH, 1863–

Knotts, Sunderland & Co.
Palatine, WV, c. 1870–1900

Krumeich, B. J.
Newark, NJ, c. 1845–60

Lambright & Westhope
New Philadelphia, OH, c. 1885–95

Lamson & Swasey
Portland, ME, 1875–c. 1884

Lathrop, Charles
Norwich, CT, 1792–

Laufersweiler, F.
New York, NY, 1876–79

Lehman, Louis
Poughkeepsie, NY, 1852–56

Lehman, Louis & Co.
New York, NY, 1858–61

Lehman & Riedinger
Poughkeepsie, NY, 1854–57

Lent, B.
Caldwell, NJ, c. 1820

Lent, G.
Troy, NY, c. 1820–24

Lessel, George
Cincinnati, OH, 1879–99

Lessel, Peter
Cincinnati, OH, 1848–52

Lessel, Peter & Bros.
Cincinnati, OH, 1852–79

Lewis, Bostwick & Cady
Fairfax, VT, 1856–

Lewis & Cady
Fairfax, VT, 1858–

Lewis & Gardiner
Huntington, NY, 1827–54

Lewis, W. A.
Galesville, NY, c. 1860

Link, Christian
Stonetown, PA, c. 1870–1900

Linton, William
Baltimore, MD, 1842–c. 1850

Lundy & Co.
W. Troy, NY, c. 1826

Lyman, Alanson & Clark, Decius
Gardiner, ME, 1837–41

Machett, I. V.
Barbadoes Neck, NJ, c. 1819–c. 1850

Machett, I. V.
Cornwall, NY, c. 1859–c. 1865

Machett, I. V. & Son
Cornwall, NY, c. 1850–c. 1859

Macomb Pottery
Macomb, IL, c. 1880–1900

MacQuoid, William & Co.
New York, NY, c. 1863–79

Madden, J. M.
Rondout, NY, c. 1870

Mantell, James & Mantell, Thomas
Penn Yan, NY, c. 1850–c. 1876

Mantell & Thomas
Penn Yan, NY, c. 1855–c. 1876

Markel, Immon & Co.
Akron, OH, 1869

Mason & Russell
Cortland, NY, 1835–39

Massilon Stoneware Co.
Massilon, OH, 1882–1900

Mayers, W. S.
Roseville, OH, c. 1870–80

McChesney, Andrew
New Philadelphia, OH, c. 1840–50

McKenzie Bros.
Vanport, PA, c. 1840–50

McLuney, Wm.
Charleston, WV, c. 1809–15

Mead, Abraham
Greenwich, CT, c. 1769–c. 1795

Mead, I. M. & Co.
Mogadore, OH, 1840–60

Merrill, E. H. & Co.
Akron, OH, 1861–

Merrill, Earl & Merrill, Ford
Mogadore, OH, c. 1880–1900

Merrill, Edwin & Merrill, Calvin
Akron, OH, 1847–61

Merrill, Edwin & Merrill, Henry E.
Akron Pottery Co.
Akron, OH, 1861–88

Metzner, Adolph
Hamilton, OH, c. 1884–c. 1900

Miller, J.
Wheeling, WV, c. 1869–80

Miner, William
Symes Creek, OH, 1869–83

Monmouth Pottery Co.
Monmouth, IL, c. 1890–1900

Monroe, J. S. and Monroe, E. D.
Mogadore, OH, 1845–80

Montell, E. A.
Olean, NY, 1870–c. 1873

Mooney, D. & Mooney, M.
Ithaca, NY, c. 1864

Moore, Alvin S.
Talmadge, OH, 1850–70

Morable, Pascal
Seagrove, NC, c. 1900–15

Morgan, David
New York, NY, c. 1795–1803

Morgan, James
Cheesequake, NJ, c. 1775–84

Morgan, James, Jr.
Cheesequake, NJ, c. 1784–1805

Morgan, James & Co.
Cheesequake, NJ, 1805–c. 1830

Myers, E. W.
Mogadore, OH, c. 1870

Myers & Hall
Mogadore, OH, c. 1873

Nash, H. & Nash G.
Utica, NY, 1832–37

Navarre Stoneware Co.
Navarre, OH, c. 1880–1900

New York Stoneware Co.
Satterlee & Morey
Fort Edward, NY, 1861–85

Nichols & Alford
Burlington, VT, 1854–56

Nichols & Boynton
Burlington, VT, 1856–c. 1860

Nichols & Co.
Burlington, VT, 1854–60

Norton, E.
Bennington, VT, 1881–83

Norton, E. & Co.
Bennington, VT, 1883–94

Norton, E. L. P.
Bennington, VT, 1883–94

Norton, Edward
Bennington, VT, 1883–94

Norton, Edward & Co.
Bennington, VT, 1883–94

Norton, Edward & Company
Bennington, VT, 1883–94

Norton & Fenton
Bennington, VT, 1844–47

Norton & Fenton
East Bennington, VT, 1844–47

Norton, J.
Bennington, VT, 1847–50

Norton, J.
East Bennington, VT, 1841–44

Norton, J. & Co.
Bennington, VT, 1859–61

Norton, J. & E.
Bennington, VT, 1850–59

Norton, J. & E. & Co.
Bennington, VT, 1859–61

Norton, John
Bennington, VT, 1793–

Norton, Julius
Bennington, VT, 1841–44

Norton, Julius
Bennington, VT, 1847–50

Norton, Julius
East Bennington, VT, 1841–44

Norton, L.
Bennington, VT, 1823–33

Norton, L. & Co.
Bennington, VT, 1823–28

Norton, L. & Son
Bennington, VT, 1833–40

Norton, L. & Son
East Bennington, VT, 1833–40

Norwich Pottery Works
Norwich, CT, 1881–95

O'Connell, R.
Albany, NY, c. 1850

Ohio Stoneware Co.
Akron, OH, c. 1887

Onondago Pottery Co.
Geddes, NY, 1871–84

Orcutt, Belding & Co.
Ashfield, MA, 1849

Orcutt, Eleazer
Albany, NY, 1842–c. 1850
Troy, NY, 1852–60

Orcutt, Humiston & Co.
Troy, NY, c. 1850–60

Orcutt, Stephen
Whately, MA, 1797–c. 1810

Orcutt, Walter
Orcutt, Guilford, & Co.
Ashfield, MA, c. 1848

Orcutt, Walter & Co.
Ashfield, MA, 1850

Ottman Bros. & Co.
Fort Edward, NY, 1872–c. 1892

Packer, T. A.
New Philadelphia, OH, c. 1875–85

Palmer, Joseph & Cranch, Richard
Braintree, MA, 1753–

Parker, Grace
Thomas Symmes & Co.
Charlestown, MA, 1742–c. 1752

Parr, David
Baltimore, MD, 1819–34

Parr, David & Parr, Margaret
Baltimore, MD, 1842–50

Parr, James L.
Maryland Pottery
Baltimore, MD, 1842–50

Peoria Pottery Co.
Peoria, IL, 1873–1902

Perine, Maulden
Baltimore, MD, 1827–1938

Perine, Peter
Baltimore, MD, c. 1793–1819

Perry, Sanford S.
Troy, NY, c. 1827–31

Pettie, Henry & Co.
Pittsburgh, PA, c. 1860

Pewtress, J. B.
Perth Amboy, NJ, c. 1840

Pewtress, S. L.
New Haven, CT, c. 1868–87

Pfaltzgraff Pottery
York, PA, c. 1840–1900

Pharris, C. E. & Co.
Geddis, NY, c. 1864–c. 1867

Phillips, Moro
Camden, NJ, 1867–97

Pierce, John, Wadhams, Jesse, & Brooks, Hervey
Kitchfield, CT, 1753–

Pierson, Andrew
Bangor Stoneware
Bangor, ME, c. 1890–1916

Pitkin, Richard & Woodbridge, Dudley
Manchester, CT, 1800–c. 1820

Plaisted, F. A.
Gardiner, ME, c. 1850–74

Porter & Fraser
West Troy, NY, 1846–73

Porter, Nathan
West Troy, NY, 1846–73

Portland Pottery Works
Portland, ME, 1881–90

Pottman Bros.
Fort Edward, NY, c. 1870

Potts, C. & Son
Norwich, CT, 1796–

Potts, Christopher & Son
Norwich, CT, 1796–97

Price, Abial
Middletown Point, NJ, 1847–52

Price, Xerxes
Roundabout Pottery
S. Amboy, NJ, c. 1802–30

Pruden, John
Elizabeth, NJ, 1816–79

Pruden, John M., Jr.
Elizabeth, NJ, 1835–79

Purdy, Fitzhugh
Mogadore, OH, c. 1860

Purdy, Gordon
Mogadore, OH, 1860–70

Purdy, Henry
Mogadore, OH, 1838–c. 1850

Purdy & Loomis
Atwater, OH, 1871

Purdy, Solomon
Mogadore, OH, 1828–c. 1840

Quigley, S.
Cincinnati, OH, c. 1834

Quinn, E. H.
Brooklyn, NY, c. 1860

Ransbottom Bros.
Roseville, OH, 1900–08

Read, Thomas
New Philadelphia, OH, c. 1850–65

Red Wing Stoneware Co.
Red Wing, MN, c. 1872–1900

Reiss, William
Wilmington, DE, c. 1851

Remmey, Henry
New York, NY, c. 1789–1800

Remmey, Henry
Philadelphia, PA, 1810–35

Remmey, Henry H.
Baltimore, MD, c. 1818–35

Remmey, John
New York, NY, c. 1736–c. 1760

Remmey, John Jr.
New York, NY, c. 1780–c. 1792

Remmey, John I.
New York, NY, 1735–

Remmey, John II
New York, NY, 1762–

Remmey, John III
New York, NY, c. 1799–1819

Remmey, Joseph Henry
South Amboy, NJ, c. 1818–24

Remmey, Richard C.
Philadelphia, PA, c. 1859–1901

Rhodes, T.
Lincolnton, NC, c. 1865–1900

Rice, Prosper
Putnam, OH, c. 1828–50

Richey & Hamilton
Palantine, WV, c. 1875

Riedinger & Caire
Poughkeepsie, NY, 1857–78

Riggs, Wesley
Sandyville, OH, c. 1820–30

Risley, George L.
Norwich, CT, c. 1875–80

Risley, Sidney
Norwich, CT, c. 1846–75

Roberts, D. & Co.
Utica, NY, 1827–28

Roberts, William
Binghamton, NY, 1848–88

Robinson, Merrill
Akron, OH, 1900–02

Roche & Co.
New York, NY, 1855–58

Roche, E.
New York, NY, 1849–50

Rogers Pottery Co.
Thomasville, GA, c. 1830–1900

Rowley, William
Middlebury, OH, 1875–83

Royer, A.
Akron, OH, c. 1865–75

Russell, Andrew J.
Troy, NY, c. 1870–78

Ryan Bros.
Ellenville, NY, c. 1875

Sables, T. & Co.
Medford, MA, 1838–c. 1845

Sage, J. & Co.
Cortland, NY, c. 1870

Sandford, Peter Peregrine
Hackensack, NJ, c. 1789

Satterlee & Morey
New York Stoneware Co.
Fort Edward, NY, 1861–65

Schenefelder, Daniel P.
Reading, PA, 1869–1900

Schenkle, William
Excelsior Pottery
Akron, OH, c. 1870–75

Schofield, D. G. & Co.
New Brighton, PA, c. 1877–93

Schrieber, John
Rondout, NY, c. 1870

Scott, Alexander F. & Co.
Boston, MA, c. 1870–95

Scott, George
Cincinnati, OH, c. 1845–89

Scott, George & Sons
Cincinnati, OH, 1889–1900

Seaver, John & William, Jr.
Taunton, MA, c. 1815–c. 1830

Seaver, William
Taunton, MA, c. 1790–1815

Selby & Colson
Poughkeepsie, NY, 1839–41

Selby, Edward
Hudson, NY, c. 1836–c. 1850

Selby, Edward & Son
West Troy, NY, c. 1876

Selby & Emigh
Poughkeepsie, NY, 1841–44

Selby & Sanderson
Poughkeepsie, NY, 1839–41

Seymour, George R.
West Troy, NY, c. 1845–60

Seymour, Israel
Troy, NY, 1819–65

Seymour, N.
Hartford, CT, 1790–c. 1842

Seymour, N. & A.
Rome, NY, 1815–c. 1850

Seymour, Nathanial
Hartford, CT, 1790–

Seymour, Orson & Webster, Charles T.
Hartford, CT, 1857–c. 1867

Seymour & Stedman
Ravenna, OH, c. 1850

Seymour, Walter
Troy, NY, 1852–c. 1885

Sheldon, F. L.
Mogadore, OH, 1845–78

Shenkle Bros. & Mann
Akron, OH, 1863–

Shepard, Joseph, Jr.
Geddes, NY, 1857–c. 1864

Shepley & Smith
West Troy, NY, c. 1865–c. 1895

Sherwood Bros. Co.
New Brighton, PA. 1877–1900

Shorb, Adam A.
Canton, OH, 1824–c. 1850

Shorb, Adam L.
Canton, OH, c. 1840–c. 1860

Shorb, J., Jr.
Canton, OH, 1817–24

Smith, Asa E.
Norwalk, CT, 1825–37

Smith, Asa E. & Sons
Norwalk, CT., 1850–87

Smith & Bricker
Albany, NY, 1843–47

Smith & Day
Norwalk, CT, 1843–c. 1850

Smith, J. C.
Mogadore, OH, c. 1860

Smith, Willoughby
Wrightstown, PA, c. 1862–1900

Smyth, Joel & Smyth, Harmell
Paris, OH, c. 1840

Snyder, Henry
Millersburg, OH, c. 1875–85

Somerset Pottery
Somerset, MA, 1847–1909

Somerset Pottery Works
Somerset, NJ, c. 1875

Souter, John
Hartford, CT, 1790–

Sowers, H.
Roseville, OH, c. 1887

Spafford & Richards
Akron, OH, 1870–

Standish, Alex & Wright, Franklin
Taunton, MA, c. 1846–70

Starkey & Howard
Keene, NH, 1871–74

States, Adam
Greenwich, CT, c. 1749–68

States, Adam
Huntington, NY, 1751–

States, Adam
Stonington, CT, c. 1767–1826

States, Peter
Stonington, CT, c. 1767

States, William
Stonington, CT, c. 1810–23

Stearns, A. S.
Stearns & Co.
Fairfax, VT, 1852–

Stedman, Absalom
New Haven, CT, c. 1825–30

Stetzenmeyer, F. & Co.
Rochester, NY, c. 1853–55

Stetzenmeyer, F. & Goetzmann, G.
Rochester, NY, 1857–c. 1860

Stoll, S. L. & Co.
Mogadore, OH, 1864–

Straw, Michael
Greensburg, PA, c. 1837

Stroup, George
Atwater, OH, 1872

Swan, Joshua & States, Ichabod
Stonington, CT, c. 1823–35

Swank, Hiram & Sons
Johnstown, PA, c. 1865–99

Swasey, E. & Co.
Portland, ME, 1890–c. 1930

Swasey, Jones & Co.
Portland, ME, 1884–86

Swasey, Lamson & Co.
Portland, ME, 1886–c. 1890

Symmes, T. & Co.
Charlestown, MA, c. 1743–c. 1746

Synan, Patrick & Synan, William
Somerset, MA, 1893–c. 1912

Taft, James S.
Keene, NH, c. 1870–c. 1880

Thayer, Pliny
Lansingburg, NY, c. 1850–c. 1857

Thomas Bros.
Cuyahoga Falls, OH, c. 1887–1900

Thomas, J. R.
Cuyahoga Falls, OH, c. 1857–87

Thompson, Greenland
Morgantown, WV, 1870–

Thompson & Tyler
Troy, NY, c. 1858–59

Titus, Jonathan
Huntington, NY, 1784–

Tourpet & Becker
Brazil, IN, c. 1859–1900

Tracy, Andrew & Tracy, Huntington
Norwich, CT, c. 1796–98

Tracy, John B.
New Philadelphia, OH, c. 1875–90

Tracy, Nelson
New Philadelphia, OH, c. 1865–75

Troy Pottery
Troy, NY, 1861–65

Tyler & Co.
Troy, NY, 1859–61

Tyler & Dillon
Albany, NY, c. 1826–c. 1834

Tyler, Moses
Albany, NY, 1826–48

Tyron, Wright & Co.
Tallmadge, OH, c. 1868–75

Uhl, A. & L.
Evansville, IN, c. 1864–87

Underwood, J. A. & Underwood, C. W.
Fort Edward, NY, c. 1865–c. 1880

Union Pottery
Newark, NJ, c. 1865–c. 1880

United States Stoneware Co.
Akron, OH, c. 1885–1900

Van Schoik, Joseph & Dunn, Ezra
Middletown, NJ, 1852–59

Van Wickle, Jacob
Cheesequake, NJ, c. 1800–c. 1830

Van Wickle, Nicholas
Herbertsville, NJ, 1823–26

Vandemark, John
Frazesburg Road, OH, c. 1840–c. 1850

Vaupel, Cornelius
Brooklyn, NY, c. 1877–94

Viall & Markel
Akron, OH, 1869–

Wagoner Bros.
Vanport, PA, c. 1860–70

Wait, Luke & Wait, Obediah
Whately, MA, c. 1810–30

Wands, I. H.
Olean, NY, 1852–70

Warne, Thomas
Cheesequake, NJ, c. 1805–14

Warne, Thomas & Letts, Joshua
Cheesequake, NJ, c. 1778–c. 1820

Warner, William E.
West Troy, NY, c. 1835–c. 1870

Watson, J. R.
Perth Amboy, NJ, c. 1833–40

Watson & Sanderson
Poughkeepsie, NY, 1839–41

Weaver, James L.
Roseville, OH, c. 1877

Webster, Charles & Seymour, Orson
Hartford, CT, 1857–c. 1867

Webster, Elijah
East Liverpool, OH, c. 1859–c. 1864

Webster, Mack C. & Goodwin, Horace
Hartford, CT, c. 1810–40

Weeks, F. H.
Akron, OH, c. 1880–1910

Weir Pottery Co.
Monmouth, IL, 1899–1906

Weise, Henry
Martinsburg, WV, c. 1870

Welker, Adam
Massilon, OH, c. 1860–85

Weller, Samuel
Fultonham, OH, c. 1873–1900

Wells, Ashbel
Hartford, CT, c. 1785–c. 1805

Wells, Joseph
Wellsville, OH, 1826–c. 1830

Wells, S.
Wellsville, OH, c. 1835–1855

West Troy Pottery
West Troy, NY, c. 1870–80

West Virginia Pottery Co.
Bridgeport, WV, 1880–1900

Western Stoneware Co.
Monmouth, IL, 1870–90

Weston, D.
Ellenville, NY, c. 1828–47

Weston & Gregg
Ellenville, NY, c. 1870

Weston, H.
Ellenville, NY, c. 1829–48

Weston, W. W. & Weston, D.
Ellenville, NY, c. 1848

White, Noah
Utica, NY, c. 1838–50

White, Noah & Co.
Binghamton, NY, 1865–68

White, Noah & Son
Utica, NY, 1880–86

White & Wood
Binghamton, NY, 1883–87

Whiteman, T. W.
Perth Amboy, NJ, c. 1860–c. 1870

Whitman, H. M.
Havana, NY, c. 1860

Whitmore, Robinson & Co.
Akron, OH, 1862–1900

Whittemore, A. O.
Havana, NY, c. 1860–c. 1880

Willard & Sons
Ballardville, MA, c. 1880–95

Williams & McCoy
Roseville, OH, 1886–1900

Wingender, Charles
Haddonfield, NJ, c. 1890–1904

Winslow, John T.
Portland, ME, c. 1846

Woodruff, Madison
Cortland, NY, 1849–c. 1885

Woolworth, F.
Burlington, VT, c. 1879–95

Wores, H.
Dover, OH, c. 1824–46

Worthen, C. F.
Peabody, MA, c. 1865

Wright, F. T. & Co.
Taunton, MA, c. 1855–68

Young, Samuel
Martin's Ferry, OH, c. 1850

Zanesville Stoneware Co.
Zanesville, OH, c. 1887

Zipf, Jacob
Union Pottery
Newark, NJ, 1877–1906

Glossary

ALBANY SLIP: A deep chocolate brown glaze used to seal the interior and exterior walls of stoneware crocks, jugs, jars, and churns. Employed by potteries in and near Albany, New York, its use dates to the late nineteenth and early twentieth centuries.

ALKALINE GLAZE: Common to the southern and southeastern United States, a type of glaze produced by combining wood ashes or lime soaked in water with sand or ground glass.

BARTMAN JUG: A Rhenish salt-glazed jug of the sixteenth and seventeenth centuries that bears the face of a bearded man in relief.

BELLARMINE: Modern day term used to identify sixteenth- and seventeenth-century bartman jugs.

BLISTERING: A swelling or bubbling that forms in the clay during firing, usually caused by overheating of the kiln.

BOLT: A log-shaped length of clay, weighing twenty or more pounds. Clay was stored in bolts for throwing.

BRISTOL GLAZE: A creamy white surface coating applied to the upper portion of crocks, jugs, churns, and other vessels that had previously been sealed with Albany slip. Developed in Bristol, England, Bristol glaze was used in the United States late in the nineteenth century.

CAPACITY MARK: A number often either stenciled or impressed on a crock, jug, or other vessel to indicate its capacity, usually in gallons.

COBALT: A metallic element that occurs in compounds that provide blue coloring substances.

COBALT BLUE: Any of a number of pigments containing an oxide of cobalt.

COGGLE, COGGLE WHEEL: A small wheel bearing a sunken or incised design that is rolled over the surface of the clay before firing to form a decoration.

CRAWLING: During firing, crawling occurs when the glaze mixture tends to form into small clumps instead of being smooth and uniform.

DASHER: In churning butter, the plunger used to agitate the cream.

EARTHENWARE: Pottery made from red clays fired at between 1,000 and 1,200 degrees centigrade (as compared to stoneware, fired at nearly 1,300 degrees centigrade).

GLAZE: The smooth, glossy surface or coating given a piece of pottery. The four most common glazes used by American potters during the nineteenth century were salt, Albany slip, Bristol, and alkaline.

GREENWARE: Vessels that have been formed by the potter and dried, but not fired.

IMPRESSING: A method of decoration in which a design is pressed into damp clay with a hand stamp or coggle.

INCISE: A technique of decoration in which a sharp-pointed instrument, such as a nail, is used to scratch the surface layer of clay after a vessel is formed, often revealing a contrasting color beneath. The technique is often called sgrafitto.

INCISING: A decorating technique in which a design is outlined in the damp clay with a nail or other sharp-pointed instrument.

KILN: The heavy-walled, brick-lined oven in which clay vessels are fired.

LINE: A very thin crack in a stoneware vessel (short for hairline).

LUG HANDLE: Common to stoneware crocks, such handles are mounted in pairs on opposite sides of the vessel, and attached to the crock side along their entire length.

MARKED: A piece of pottery bearing the name of the potter. Often impressed into the surface of a vessel with printer's type, the maker's mark usually includes not only the potter's name but location of the pottery.

OCHER: An earthy mineral oxide of iron which, when combined with clay and sand, produces a reddish or brownish mixture.

OVOID: A vessel with broad shoulders tapering to a smaller base; pear-shaped.

PINHOLES: Tiny holes that appear in the glaze, caused by escaping gases during firing.

POPOUT: A defect in a stoneware vessel that results when particules of lime in the clay burst open during firing.

PORRINGER: A small-handled bowl or cup.

PUG MILL: A cylinder-shaped vat in which raw clay is refined and mixed.

REDWARE: A type of pottery made from the same common red-burning clays used in the manufacture of bricks and roof tiles. Redware was produced from as early as the 1630s until the 1920s.

RHEINLAND: That part of Germany west of the Rhine River; also Rhineland.

RHENISH: Pertaining to the regions bordering the Rhine River.

RIB: A wooden scraper used by the potter for smoothing the sides and forming the rims of stoneware vessels.

ROCKINGHAM: A type of glazed brown-and-yellow mottled earthenware, often used for teapots, pitchers, and other household articles. The term is also applied to a type of early and elegant porcelain.

SALT GLAZE: The smooth glossy surface on stoneware pieces that results from vaporization of salt during the firing process.

SGRAFITTO: A technique of decoration in which a mark or design is incised into the surface of a piece of pottery.

SLIP: A creamy mixture of clay and water used in pottery decoration.

SLIP CUP: The container used in applying slip.

SLIP-CUPPING, SLIP-TRAILING: A decorating technique in which a cup filled with slip is used to produce a raised line, or "trail," of cobalt blue on the surface of a piece of pottery.

SLUMP: Term used when a clay vessel sags or droops in the kiln because of overfiring.

SPRIGGING: A decorating technique in which molded pieces of clay are added to a newly formed piece of pottery for ornamentation.

STONEWARE: Pottery produced from a special clay that is fired only once, but at such high temperature (from 1,200 to 1,300 degrees centigrade) that it becomes vitrified.

STRAP HANDLE: A free-standing handle formed of a looped band of clay.

SWAG: A decoration that gives the appearance of a suspended wreath, drapery, or the like.

THROWER: The specialist who "throws" the clay upon the wheel, then forms the piece; the potter.

TOBACCO SPIT: Slang term for alkaline glaze.

VITRIFICATION: The process in the kiln in which silica and other ingredients in the clay take on a glasslike quality.

WHEEL: The circular disk, mounted horizontally, which is rotated by the potter in the making of stoneware pieces.

YELLOWWARE: A type of pottery produced from yellow clays finer than earthenware clays and lighter in weight than those used in stoneware manufacture. Produced in New Jersey, Pennsylvania, Kentucky, and Ohio, yellowware was produced from the early 1850s to the mid-1920s.

Index

About the Author

George Sullivan, a free-lance writer and the author of a good number of nonfiction books, often writes about collecting and collectibles. *The Complete Book of Baseball Collectibles* and *Making Money in Autographs* are among his titles.

For this book, Mr. Sullivan interviewed stoneware dealers and collectors throughout New England and in the mid-Atlantic states. His own collection, he says, numbers about a dozen pieces that represent the work of Massachusetts potters.

Mr. Sullivan was born in Lowell, Massachusetts, and brought up in Springfield. He recalls that, in his boyhood homes, stoneware crocks and other vessels were often used on a day-to-day basis. No one thought of them as worthwhile collectibles. "Of course, no one thought baseball cards had any value, either," he says.

A graduate of Fordham University, Mr. Sullivan worked in public relations in New York City before becoming a free-lance writer. He lives in New York City with his wife. He is a member of PEN, the Authors Guild, and the American Society of Journalists and Authors.